Suez and Sinai

Harry Browne

Longman

Longman Group Limited
London

Associated companies, branches and repesentatives throughout the world

First published 1971

ISBN 0 582 32812 8

Photoset and printed in Malta
by St Paul's Press Ltd

Contents

Foreword

In the past, History traditionally has suffered as a subject from the distance placed between the student and the events themselves by the historian's own account—the interpretation of evidence in textbook, specialised account or article. This series is intended to supplement the account given by the historian with a presentation of the documents themselves so as to enable the student to form his own opinion based upon the evidence. This open-ended approach will allow the student to consider the material from which historical judgements are made and to examine critically the contemporary reaction to the events themselves.

Each contributor in the series will consider a major crisis in history and examine its complexities by means of selected documents and a short commentary. Each teacher is likely to have his own idea of how to make the best use of the material in each book. However, as an appendix to each volume, the author, while making no attempt to sum up, will suggest some of the problems which arise from the historical evidence within the documents. A full list of sources of documents appears in the Appendix to each volume, and where relevant a glossary is also given.

HARRY BROWNE
Series editor

Acknowledgements

We are grateful to the following for permission to reproduce copyright material: the Proprietors of *Associated Newspapers Ltd* for extracts from *The Daily Sketch* 1st November 1956; B.B.C. for extracts from the daily Summary of World Broadcasts published by the B.B.C. Monitoring Service; the author and the B.B.C. for extracts from *Suez Ten Years After* by Peter Calvocoressi; Cassell & Co. Ltd., and Houghton Mifflin Co. for extracts from *Full Circle* by Sir Anthony Eden; Chatto and Windus Ltd., for extracts from *Britain's Moment in the Middle East* by Elizabeth Monroe; Constable Publishers and Clarkson N. Potter for extracts from *No End of a Lesson* by Anthony Nutting; Department of State, Washington for extracts from the *Department of State Bulletin*; General Services Administration, Washington for extracts from the *Public Papers of the Presidents of the United States*; the Proprietors of *The Guardian* for extracts dated 1st and 2nd November, 1956; Her Majesty's Stationery Office for 'Statistics of Usage for 1949 and 1959, charts 2 and 3' from *Suez Canal: Annual Returns of Shipping and Tonnage* 1956 and extracts from *Hansard* Vols. 557, 558 and 561; George G. Harrop and Clarke, Irwin & Co. Ltd. for extracts from *Between Arab and Israeli* by Lieutenant-General E.L.M. Burns © 1962 by Clarke, Irwin and Company Limited. Used by permission; William Heinemann Ltd., and Doubleday & Co. Inc., for extracts from *The White House Years: Waging Peace* by Dwight D. Eisenhower; William Heinemann Ltd., and Quadrangle Books for extracts from *Dulles Over Suez* by Herman Finer copyright © 1964 by Herman Finer; author and author's agents for extracts from *The Road to Suez* by E. Childers; Hodder and Stoughton Ltd., and Coward-McCann, Inc. for extracts from *Clean Young Englishman* by John Gale, copyright © 1965 by John Gale; the Embassy of Israel for extracts from 'Voice of Zion' broadcast on 30th October 1956 by the Israel in English service; the Proprietors of the *New Statesman* for extracts from 'The Face of Intervention' from the *New Statesman* 29.12.56.; the Proprietors of *The New York Times* for extracts from 'Crisis in the Middle East'' 21st October, 1956 and ''War in the Middle East'' November, 1956 © 1956 by *The New York Times Company*. Reprinted by permission; the Proprietors of *The Observer* for extracts dated 4th and 11th November, 1956; Oxford University Press for extracts from 'Suez Canal Company Nationalization Law' from *Documents on International Affairs 1956* and Documents on International Affairs 1956 edited by Noble Frankland; the Palestine Liberation Organization Research Center for extracts from *Zionist Colonialism in Palestine* by F. A. Sayegh; Stanford University Press for extracts from *One Day in the World's Press* by Wilbur Schramm with the permission of the publishers, Stanford University Press © 1959 by the Board of Trustees of the Leland Stanford Junior University; Syndication International for extracts from the *Daily Herald* dated 1st November, 1956 by Allen Andrews; the Proprietors of *The Times Newspapers Ltd.*, for extracts from *The Times* dated 1st August 1956 and 27th August 1956; the United Arab Republic for excerpts from broadcast Press comment: Cairo in Arabic Home Service 31st October, 1956 and excerpts from radio statement by President Nasser: Cairo in Arabic Home Service 1st November, 1956; George Weidenfeld & Nicolson Ltd., and Harper & Row Publishers Inc. extracts from *Suez* by Hugh Thomas. Copyright © 1966, 1967 by Hugh Thomas and *Diary of the Sinai Campaign* by Major-General Moshe Dayan. Copyright © 1965 by Moshe Dayan. Copyright © 1966 in the English translation by George Weidenfeld and Nicolson Ltd.

We have been unable to trace the copyright holder of *Diplomacy in the Near and Middle East* by Hurewitz; and *The Weekend War* by S. Barer and would appreciate any information that would enable us to do so.

Background

1 · An International Waterway

The Suez Canal

Exactly one hundred years ago in 1869 the French Empress Eugénie aboard the imperial yacht, *L'Aigle*, set sail from Alexandria to Port Said, formally to open the new wonder of the world, the Suez Canal, the work of that many-talented man, Ferdinand de Lesseps. Today for the second time within eleven years the Suez Canal stands empty apart from marooned ships, and hostile armies bombard each other across its waters.

To close the Canal robs the maritime nations of the world of a speedy and cheap passage from the Mediterranean to the Indian Ocean and thence to Australia, Malaysia and New Zealand: it also robs Egypt of a prime source of income. In 1965 President Nasser said 'One new source alone of foreign currency, the Suez Canal, affords an income equal to the sole income on which the Egyptian economy relied before the Revolution—the cotton crop'. Before the Egyptians nationalised the Canal in 1956, the owning Company, the Universal Canal Company made in the previous year £11 million profit of which £4¼m. went to Great Britain.

Although the Canal came increasingly to be seen as almost a British preserve—even though the Company's headquarters remained in Paris—the Canal owed nothing to British enterprise or capital. Indeed if Britain had had her way, it might never have been built. From its beginnings it was a tribute to French skills and enterprise. Ferdinand de Lesseps, whose vigour and foresight, diplomatic skill, commercial and engineering enterprise made the Canal, had had a long connection with Egypt. His father Mathieu de Lesseps had been made Consul in Egypt in 1801 and witnessed the rise of the founder of modern Egypt, Mohamed Ali, who from 1805 to 1849 did much by his energy to create an Egypt independent of the Ottoman Empire. In 1832 Ferdinand renewed the family connection with Egypt when he returned as vice-consul to Alexandria. He became a close friend not only of Mohamed Ali but of Said, his son.

For de Lesseps it was a stroke of good fortune when within five years two of Mohamed Ali's sons died and Said succeeded them as Egypt's ruler. De Lesseps, now in France, hurried back to Egypt to try to convince his old friend of the potential value of his dream of a canal, piercing the Isthmus of Suez, which had for so long seized hold of his imagination. On 30 November, 1854, the first Firman of Concession was granted to de Lesseps. On 5 January 1856, a public company committed to building the Canal, the Universal Suez Canal Company, published its statutes.

De Lesseps intended from the start that of the 400,000 shares, slightly more than half (207,000) would be held by French investors but he earmarked shares for Britain, the United States, Russia and Austria. In the event none of these states invested money. The British government was frankly hostile. Palmerston, briefed by Robert Stephenson, the rail engineer who advocated an alternative rail link, spoke about the Canal in the Commons in 1857:

'It is an undertaking which, I believe, as regards its commercial character, may be deemed to rank among the many bubble schemes that from time to time have been palmed off upon gullible capitalists. I believe it is physically impracticable, except at an expense which would be far too great to warrant the expectation of any returns. The scheme is one hostile to the interests of this country. . . . The obvious political tendency of the undertaking is to render more easy the separation of Egypt from Turkey. It is founded also on remote speculation with regard to easier access to our Indian possessions. . . .'

One farsighted English shipping firm, P and O, had seen the value of the Canal—and in fact their liner *Delta* followed *L'Aigle* on the opening day. However when the Canal was working and it was increasingly clear that Britain was likely to be the greatest beneficiary, hostility still lingered despite the fact that in the first year two thirds of the transit fees had been paid by British shipping. The GPO took the view that mails carried on the Canal were not safe and until 1874 the P and O liners who carried the mails were forced to drop them at Alexandria and pick them up again at the end of the Canal, a typically British tragi-comedy.

Clearly the change in Britain's attitude to the Canal came with Disraeli's famous purchase of the Khedive Ismail's shares, 177,642 of them, at a cost of four million pounds. This investment in Canal stock was a financial prelude to Britain's military action in 1882 in occupying Egypt, an involvement in Egyptian affairs which lasted down to the removal of the last British forces in 1955. In two World Wars Britain's Middle Eastern strategy turned on the defence of the Canal and the route to India.

Britain's paternal attitude to Egypt, her long experience in Egyptian politics, the central part played by the Suez Canal in her imperial and post-imperial thinking, all these help in part to explain her readiness to intervene in Egypt again in 1956.

1 · The 1888 Convention governing the Suez Canal · Constantinople, 19 October 1888

In the name of Almighty God, Her Majesty the Queen of the United Kingdom of Great Britain and Ireland, Empress of India; His Majesty the Emperor of Germany, King of Prussia; His Majesty the Emperor of Austria, King of Bohemia etc., and Apostolic King of Hungary; His Majesty the King of Spain, and in His name the Queen Regent of the Kingdom; the President of the French Republic; His Majesty the King of Italy; His Majesty the King of the Netherlands, Grand Duke of Luxembourg, etc., His Majesty the Emperor of the Russians; and His Majesty the Emperor of the Ottomans;

Wishing to establish, by a Conventional Act, a definite system destined to guarantee at all times and for all the Powers, the free use of the Suez Maritime Canal, and thus to complete the system under which the navigation of this Canal has been placed by the Firman of his Imperial Majesty the Sultan dated the 22 February, 1866, and sanctioning the Concessions of His Highness the Khedive,

Have agreed upon the following Articles:

Article 1 . The Suez Maritime Canal shall always be free and open, in time of war as in time of peace, to every vessel of commerce or of war, without distinction of flag.

Consequently the High Contracting Parties agree not in any way to interfere with the free use of the Canal, in time of war as in time of peace.

The Canal shall never be subjected to the exercise of the right of blockade.

Article 2. The High Contracting Parties, recognising that the Fresh-Water Canal is indispensable to the Maritime Canal, take note of the engagements of His Highness the Khedive towards the Universal Suez Canal Company as regards the Fresh-Water Canal; which engagements are stipulated in a Convention bearing the date of 18 March 1863, containing an expose and four Articles.

They undertake not to interfere in any way with the security of that Canal and its branches, the working of which shall not be exposed to any attempt at obstruction.

Article 3. The High Contracting Parties likewise undertake to respect the plant, establishments, buildings and works of the Maritime Canal and of the Fresh-Water Canal.

Article 4. The Maritime Canal remaining open in time of war as a free passage, even to the ships of war of belligerents, according to the terms of Article 1 of the present Treaty, the High Contracting Parties agree that no right of war, no act of hostility, nor any act having for its object to obstruct the free navigation of the Canal shall be committed in the Canal and its ports of access, as well as within a radius of three marine miles from those parts, even though the Ottoman Empire should be one of the belligerent Powers.

2 · Statistics of Usage for 1949 and 1959

2. *Traffic by Nationality (Gross and Net Tonnage)*†
(Year 1949)

Nationality	Vessels	Gross tonnage	Net tonnage
United Kingdom	3,952	34,185,907	24,883,987
United States of America	1,098	11,722,079	8,894,961
Norwegian	1,187	10,583,156	8,030,623
Panamanian	815	8,054,135	6,069,399
French	742	7,372,331	5,298,675
Italian	783	6,044,157	4,461,901
Netherlands	551	5,188,174	3,812,524
Swedish	287	2,527,070	1,920,745
Danish	235	1,871,935	1,389,529
Greek	231	1,691,013	1,256,073
Liberian	50	879,825	684,426
Honduranean	58	631,461	477,014
Egyptian	148	486,429	347,381
Belgian	46	329,799	287,237
Soviet Union	56	274,076	201,890
Turkish	42	264,175	191,765
Spanish	34	247,279	177,379
Portuguese	23	174,301	135,136
Finnish	17	150,438	102,785
Yugoslav	15	102,582	76,200
Polish	9	62,977	46,347
Chinese	7	47,473	33,024
Indian	5	30,523	22,586
Iranian	5	29,966	21,432
Argentine	2	16,051	11,803
German	1	9,085	6,538
Moroccan	1	7,245	5,367
Uruguayan	1	7,164	5,062
Saudi Arabian	9	9,331	3,939
Pakistani	3	5,622	2,686
Swiss	1	3,139	1,915
Burmese	4	1,228	657
Costa Rican	2	1,278	562
	10,420	93,064,404	68,861,548

†The figures are computed according to the official flag of the vessels, without taking into account the nationality of the owners or charterers.

3. *Traffic by Nationality (Percentage of Number and Tonnage of Vessels in Transit)*†
(Year 1949)

Nationality	Percentage of vessels	Percentage of gross tonnage	Percentage of net tonnage
United Kingdom	37·93	36·73	36·14
United States of America	10·54	12·60	12·92
Norwegian	11·39	11·37	11·66
Panamanian	7·82	8·65	8·81
French	7·12	7·92	7·69
Italian	7·51	7·49	6·48
Netherlands	5·29	5·57	5·54
Swedish	2·75	2·72	2·79
Danish	2·25	2·01	2·02
Greek	2·22	1·82	1·82
Liberian	0·48	0·95	0·99
Honduranean	0·56	0·68	0·69
Egyptian	1·42	0·52	0·50
Belgian	0·44	0·42	0·42
Soviet Union	0·54	0·29	0·29
Turkish	0·40	0·28	0·28
Spanish	0·32	0·27	0·26
Portuguese	0·22	0·19	0·20
Finnish	0·16	0·16	0·15
Yugoslav	0·14	0·11	0·11
Polish	0·09	0·07	0·07
Chinese	0·07	0·05	0·05
Indian	0·05	0·03	0·03
Iranian	0·05	0·03	0·03
Argentine	0·02	0·02	0·02
German	0·01	0·01	0·01
Moroccan	0·01	0·01	0·01
Uruguayan	0·01	0·01	0·01
Saudi Arabian	0·09	0·01	0·01
Pakistani	0·03	0·01	(0·004)
Swiss	0·01	(0·003)	(0·003)
Burmese	0·04	(0·001)	(0·001)
Costa Rican	0·02	(0·001)	(0·001)
	100	100	100

†The figures are computed according to the official flag of the vessels, without taking into account the nationality of the owners or charterers.

2 · The Arab–Israeli Confiict

Origins of Israel

Today Arab nationalism stands pitted against the nationalism of the new state of the Jews, Israel. Across the now disused Suez Canal Egyptian faces Israeli. In the air Israeli and Egyptian fighters engage in sporadic gun battles. Palestinian guerillas plant bombs in Israeli supermarkets, hi-jack planes with Israeli passengers, machine-gun Israeli planes taxiing on foreign runways. In response, Israel carries out large scale retaliation with attacks on Arab guerilla bases or commando raids such as the attack on all Arab planes on Beirut airport over Christmas of 1968.

These two now bitterly-opposed nationalisms are both products of the nineteenth century, growing up almost simultaneously. In 1882, the first *Aliyah*, Jewish pioneers, fourteen men and one woman, landed at Jaffa and marked the beginning of modern Jewish immigration into Palestine. In Beirut, in 1875, at the Syrian Protestant College the first Arab nationalist secret society was founded, committed to ridding Arab lands of the Turks. Intellectual developments were also paralleled. In 1913 the Vienna Zionist Congress had decided on setting up a Hebrew University in Jerusalem. Both in Beirut and Constantinople Arab literary and intellectual societies were in the making. For the Arab the need was to stir up their brothers to free their lands of the alien Turk; for the Jew to create a homeland of their own in the traditional heartlands of Jewry for already strident European nationalisms were making the Jew a stranger even in those lands such as the German-speaking countries where he was most closely integrated.

Britain's declaration to the Jews, the Balfour Declaration, in November 1917, had opened up the possibility of extensive Jewish immigration into Palestine and the creation of a national home. At the same time in the McMahon letters addressed to Hussein, Grand Sharif of Mecca and head of the Arab movement against the Turks, Britain had promised the Arabs independence in their own homelands. These promises were contradictory and were never to be resolved. The land of Palestine was mandated to Britain in the Versailles Settlement and Britain honoured the Balfour Declaration by allowing Jewish immigrants into Palestine. However Jews did not flock into Palestine in the twenties and the British government began to wonder if it might not be better discreetly to bury Balfour's Declaration in order to maintain a friendly relationship with the Arab world, on which so much seemed to depend, particularly the safety of traffic through the Suez Canal.

In the inter-war years the Arabs refused steadily to negotiate with successive British governments and would not consider even the now fashionable proposal for a bi-national state. The shape of the Palestine problem was transformed by the rise of Hitler in 1933. His savage and unremitting persecution of German Jewry led in turn to increased immigration into Palestine. The Arabs responded by a general strike and armed rebellion (1936) and Britain in the White Paper of 1939 announced what was the virtual abandonment of Balfour, restricted Jewish immigration for the next five years and then a transfer of immigration control to the Arabs.

The Nazi attack upon German and then European Jewry, the murder of six million Jews hardened Jewish certainty that there was no future with the *goyim*, only with their own kind in their own land. Large scale Jewish immigration into Palestine began again at the end of the war, much of it illegal, and a Britain riven by economic difficulties could find no answer short of imprisoning the illegals in Cyprus or returning them to Germany itself. By this unthought-out policy, Britain lost world sympathy, particularly that of the USA, more ready with advice than help. Britain's own patience was strained by the activities of Jewish terrorist bands, Irgun and the Stern Gang, which made the Mandate even harder to shoulder. In 1947 Britain's Foreign Secretary, Ernest Bevin, passed the whole problem of Palestine back to the authority responsible for the Mandate, the United Nations, the successor to the League of Nations.

Both in America and in the UN there was increasing support for the idea of an independent Jewish state and in 1947 the United Nations declared for partition in Palestine, with a separate Arab and separate Jewish state (29 November 1947). The Arabs rejected partition immediately; the Jews accepted the idea. Meanwhile the British made speed to move out on their appointed day, 15 May 1948, leaving behind them no successor authority to take responsibility. On that day official war between Arab and Israeli began although in fact fighting had been going on for some months. The crack Arab army, the Jordan Arab Legion attacked Jerusalem; the Egyptians, Syrians, Iraquis all invaded the territory which the UN partition plan had ceded to the Jews. The result was the total Arab disaster of 1948, the Arab defeat in the First Arab–Israeli War.

Despite the massed forces of the Arab world, the state of Israel had been born. The Israelis, up to 1948 willing to negotiate any settlement which allowed them the right to exist now showed themselves increasingly intransigent. The proposed UN partition frontiers, rejected by the Arabs, were now no longer accepted by the Jews and during 1948 their frontiers were extended beyond the original demarcation lines to take in the Negev.

Causes of Tension

To the Arabs, Israel is a temporary phenomenon, the invasion of lands, traditionally Arab, by an alien culture, supported by outsiders. There is no Israel, only Palestine. The Weizmann–Feisal concept, advanced at the end of the First World War of 'Semitic brothers' was answered in 1946 by the then Secretary of the Arab League in conversation with the Labour MP, R. H. S. Crossman.

'Our brother has gone to Europe and to the West and come back something else. He has come back a Russified Jew, a Polish Jew, a German Jew, an English Jew. He has come back with a totally different conception of things, western and not eastern. That does not mean that we are necessarily quarelling with anyone who comes from the West. But the Jew, our old cousin, coming back with imperialistic ideas and trying to implement them first by British pressure and then by American pressure, and then by terrorism on his own part—he is not the old cousin, and we do not extend to him a very good welcome. The Zionist, the new Jew, wants to dominate, and he pretends that he has got a particular civilising mission with which he returns to a backward, degenerate race in order to put the elements of progress into an area which has no progress. Well, that has been the pretension of every power that wanted to colonise and aimed at domination. The excuse has always been that the people are backward and that he has got a human mission to put them forward . . . the Arabs simply stand and say "NO".'

Like other crusader states, Israel, seen through Arab eyes, is not a natural growth: she represents the outcome of policies of those Western Powers who first created her and then protected her. To the Arab, the much-vaunted western concept, the right of self-determination, has in Palestine been brutally cast aside, for Arabs were clearly the majority. The Arabs brush aside as irrelevant the Jewish claim that historically this was their land, that their civilisation was nurtured here. 'Our brother went away. . . . There is no Palestine problem—there is the problem of foreign occupation and foreign power.' To the Arab, 'Europeans' have once again colonised a 'non-European' area; 'Europeans' have been forced out of Kenya, out of Algeria: they will also be expelled from Palestine. Israel to the Arab is another Rhodesia and time is against them both.

Nasser is often thought to speak for the Arab world and he has many times defined the Arab view of Israel. In 1960 he declared 'Israel does not merely imply those who raped Palestine and entrenched themselves there for ever after having massacred its lawful population. Israel also means the force of evil and treachery and a colonialist conspiracy to stamp out Arabism. Israel further signifies a colonialist conspiracy fifth column, which is used at the opportune moment, as was done in 1956.' At another point he said: 'it represents a new series of crusades, directed towards Arab nationalism'. Israel, the spearhead of a great conspiracy, the instrument of the Great Powers.

Such rampant evil suggests only one solution 'we are determined to restore our rights by our own hand and power. Colonialism and Zionism must be eradicated.' To the Arabs, up to 1967, extermination was the official, much publicised answer. Since the June war, Arab propaganda offers the Jews a chance to be a minority in an Arab state.

To some Israelis, part of the Weizmann–Feisal tradition of Semitic brothers still remains. In part perhaps this is necessity—after all one tenth of Israel's population is Arab and Israel makes a conscientious attempt at integration. Sometimes a less attractive tone marks Israel's relations with her own Arabs. Ben Gurion has expressed the older view in this way:

'These two Semitic peoples, Jews and Arabs, share one mission in this corner of the world. The Jew will not budge hence, nor will the Arab change his place. History has pronounced us neighbours; and it is not merely a geographical proximity. There is much nearness in language, culture and history. Co-operation between the Jewish people in its Land and independent Arabia is an historical necessity, and it will come about, for the Arab peoples need it no less than does Israel. It is feasible only on a basis of equality, mutual respect and reciprocal aid. It will convert the Middle East into one of the cultural centres of the world, as in Bible times it was. Each of the two peoples has something to offer the other, without giving up anything of its own. The fertilising exchange will be a boon to both, to the Middle East and to the whole world.'

This splendid vision of the future awakened no echoes in the Arab world—except from Bourguiba of Tunisia. Perhaps, as Ben Gurion argues, it will have to wait on the formation of liberal, democratic governments among the Arabs.

The influx of Jews from North Africa, from the Yemen, Jews from Arab lands—has made Israel less and less obviously a Western state in appearance. Some influential Israelis in stressing Israel's deep roots in the Middle East, point also to the 'orientalisation' of the state. Israel in this view is not an intruder, not a thorn in the Arab side. She is a Middle Eastern state among other Middle East states.

In reality the Middle East remains for the Arab a region where time since 1948 has stood still and no state of Israel exists; for the Israeli it is an area in which life is lived in permanent siege conditions; for both, a place of sudden death, of terror raids, of intermittent war.

The Arab–Israeli dispute afflicts the area in many ways, the Arab boycott the most persistent and pervasive. It began immediately after the Second World War with the Arab League, the organisation of Arab states, calling on its members to bar the entry of goods made by Palestine Jews. This boycott came into force on 1 January 1946.

When Israel fought her way to nationhood in 1948, the Arabs intensified their boycott. In all Arab capitals, Cairo, Alexandria, Baghdad, Beirut, Tripoli and Amman, the Damascus central boycott office set up a branch, coercing Arab traders into taking part. The Arab League tightened its control of Israel's trade in 1950, drawing up a 'black list' of all ships calling at Israeli ports. The Arabs banned any such ship from their own ports and even from servicing in Arab harbours. Maritime countries soon accepted the boycott: the alternative was clear. Ships bound for Israel putting in at Arab ports were not only blacklisted but Israeli cargo was confiscated. Governments affected have never made joint protest against unlawful confiscation or Arab invasion of legitimate trading rights.

Arab success at sea has been matched by Arab triumph in the air.

Israel's international airport, Lydda, once served lines operating to Calcutta, Karachi, Colombo, Tokyo and Manila, to Asia and Far Eastern airports. To fly to the East from Lydda involved crossing Arab territory in Iraq, Jordan or Saudi Arabia. The boycott was extended to include airspace. Israel was forbidden to fly across Arab lands. In 1955 the Israeli airline El Al was warned that if her planes flew over the Tiran Straits Egypt would fire on them.

The excessive caution of the shipping companies and their protector governments was matched by the airlines. Companies cancelled services, rerouted planes through Cairo and Beirut. Israel's business men could not fly from Lydda to the Far East until 1956, when Air France set up a service from Lydda to Teheran and beyond to Tokyo and the Far East. How rapidly opposition can change the Arab viewpoint the world saw in 1954 when some Arab states barred airlines using Lydda from using Arab airports. Vigorous and unified protest produced a climbdown within a week—it had apparently all been a mistake.

Arabs have rapidly extended the boycott until it now reaches out to firms who do business with Israel and who as a consequence find themselves excluded from Arab markets. This was aimed particularly at firms with branches in Israel and some companies have been forced to abandon the Israel trade for the sake of the Arab market.

The Arab states through the boycott make Israel a pariah in the Middle East: it is a constant strain on her ingenuity, and on her economy. It does not perhaps create as much continual friction as the bitter quarrel over the Jordan waters. The key to agricultural progress in the Middle East is water, water for irrigation, water for power. States in the Fertile Crescent can never have a High Dam to fertilise and power the region for there is no Nile. (The Nile's annual flow is 84,000 million cubic metres; the Jordan, 1,880 mcm.) No-one expects political agreement which would make possible harmonious co-operation in any major water scheme. Under the mandate no important scheme was started; since the war and in particular since 1948 the four independent states in the area, with Israel as one of the states concerned, have never reached agreement on anything. Arabs will not negotiate with Israel; joint committees of all four states are therefore impossible.

In 1954 President Eisenhower sent out a special envoy, Eric Johnston, a persistent and skilled negotiator, who, working separately with Israel and the Arab states, produced a scheme to provide water for the region through the use of the waters of the river Jordan. There were several special features of the Jordan water which both complicated and eased the problem of harnessing its waters. 'Jordan' means 'the downcomer' and the river's fall enables its gravity flow to be widely used. Again Lake Tiberias provides a splendid natural storage basin. Such a storage basin is made essential by the nature of the Jordan's intake: three of the four main streams feeding the Jordan are rain or snow-fed and the greater part of their annual flow comes down in the winter spate. The main disadvantage of the water is its salt content. When it enters Tiberias, the river is sweet: when it leaves salt springs around the Lake have forced up its salt content to 270 parts of salt per million cubic metres. Above 170 p.p.m. oranges may suffer immediate damage.

Eric Johnston's plan awarded 60 per cent of the Jordan waters to the Arab states, the remainder to Israel. The slim possibility of co-operation was wrecked by the worsening of relations in 1956 leading finally to the Israel–Egyptian war.

By far the most tragic problem dividing the Arab world from Israel is the fact and plight of the Arab refugees. How many there are has been differently estimated—an official letter from the Arab League in *The Times* (29 May 1967) gave the figure of 1½ million. In 1958, however, the responsible United Nations agency, UNRWA gave a figure of 963,000. By far the largest number are in Jordan (539,000) and the Gaza Strip (225,000) and the remainder are in Lebanon and Syria.

What may well be asked is: do they wish to return? In the years after the Arab–Israeli war of 1948 the United Nations tried to secure the return of those who wished to go. The UN set up a Palestine Conciliation Commission, charged amongst other tasks with fulfilling the expressed wish of the General Assembly's resolution of 11 December 1948 which ran:

'that the refugees wishing to return to their homes and live at peace with their neighbours should be permitted to do so at the earliest practicable date, and that compensation should be paid for the property of those choosing not to return, and for the loss of or damage to property which, under principles of international law or in equity, should be made good by the Government or authorities responsible.'

The Conciliation Commission called a conference on the neutral ground of Lausanne, attended by Arab and Israeli representatives. There was, of course, no direct negotiations. Arabs will not sit and bargain with Israelis. Israel proposed taking over the Gaza Strip and assuming responsibility for the refugees living there. This the Arabs looked on as fresh evidence of Israel's imperialism and no more was heard of this scheme. However some progress was made for the Arabs agreed to discuss the UN Partition Plan of 29 November 1947 as a basis for negotiations. This in itself was a major step forward as it implied Arab willingness to recognise the political fact of Israel's existence.

No solution for the refugee problem emerged from Lausanne. Israel was, perhaps, understandably cautious. There was the physical difficulty: many Arab villages and houses had been destroyed in war. Where would returning refugees go? A greater sensitivity to the plight of the Arab refugees in the immediate post-war years might have helped to ease one of the most potent sources of bitterness in the Middle East. The Israelis went a little way after 1949 to carry through a limited repatriation scheme by allowing heads of Arab families in Israel to bring back wives and unmarried children. In Israel this could be seen as a humanitarian attempt to reunite tragically divided families. By Arab standards, however, the definition of a family was extremely narrow for no provision was made for brothers and sisters. Only about 38,000 Arabs returned to Israel under this scheme.

In the main, Arab countries have steadfastly refused to integrate refugees into their economy and society. Such a policy, as they see it, would imply acceptance of Israel. The slogan 'repatriation' provides a useful reason for doing nothing at all. One day they will return to their native lands. . . . Nevertheless within this broad framework, the attitudes of host countries vary from stubborn resentment to a tolerant co-operativeness.

What may also be true is that when the great Arab exodus ended in 1948 Israel often made sure that refugees would have little to come back to, for Arab villages were on occasion arbitrarily destroyed by the Israeli army. This wilful destruction of Arab property has done nothing to ease relations between Aràb and Israeli. It has, however, helped to make the question of genuine repatriation academic. In 1949, a Jewish writer, (quoted by Gabbay) described the Israeli scene:

'In Jerusalem, Jaffa, Haifa, Safed, Tiberias, Acre and Ramleh Arabs owned many modern houses. As a result of the great onrush of Jewish immigrants during the last nine months, all houses fit for habitation have inevitably been taken over. Today, Katamon, the purely Arab quarter of Jerusalem, Ein Karen, a township outside of Jerusalem, the new city of Acre, and many modern sections of Jaffa, are inhabited by Jews to full capacity. The slum sections in most of these cities have either been destroyed by warfare or dynamited in order to clear the way for proper city planning. About thirty blocks of houses in Jaffa, adjoining Tel-Aviv now present a mass of ruins and masonry, while a similar picture is to be seen in the Arab parts of Haifa. In other words, there is not a house in the cities of Israel which is free to accommodate its pre-war owners, should they return. The same is true of the bigger and more prosperous villages.'

Behind the Israeli resistance to the demand for repatriation stands primarily the concept of the rebirth and destiny of Israel. If Israel is to welcome returning exiles, if Jews throughout the world are to be 'ingathered', then there must be space within the tiny state of Israel. It would be impracticable to try to make room for a million returning Arabs, disastrously altering at the same time the balance between Jew and Arab in Israel. In the view of right-wing parties such as Herut the Arab minority already represent an intractable problem for Israel: for security and for political reasons the potential area of discontent must not be increased by encouraging the return of the refugees. After all, the Arab world is large enough to hold them. . . .

In general, Israel has been prepared to discuss separately the question of compensation for Arab losses. Arab property was not confiscated but put under the control of a Custodian of Absentee Property in 1948. Two years later the Custodian was legally empowered to sell property belonging to absentees. Parallel to this, Israel appointed a Development Authority with the sole right to buy property of absentees, a right sometimes abused—when

Arabs had been compulsorily transferred by the Israeli Army, their land was declared absentee property.

More recently, Israel's willingness to pay compensation has been tempered by circumstances unrelated to the actual value of the property. In discussing compensation, Moshe Sharett has argued in the Knesset that any figure arrived at would have to take into account the effect of the Arab boycott and Israel's need for a heavy military budget, forced on her by Arab hostility.

The Arab refugees represent a charge on the international conscience, a standing criticism of Israel and the Arabs. Their case awaits a general pacification of the Middle East. In the meantime their only hope is resettlement in other Arab lands. For the young and able this is already happening, for Palestinian Arabs can be found in most Arab countries as for instance, teachers, clerks, or technicians: for the older refugees the immediate need is to save many of them from life as a permanent camp inmate.

Israel and the Arab League had continually protested that violence was far from their minds. In a striking phrase, David Ben Gurion, the founding father of Israel and Prime Minister during the Suez crisis, affirmed 'Israel has never had, and never will have, aggressive intentions against anyone. Israel's hand is extended in peace to all the Arab states.' Those Arab states who so recently had invaded Palestine now roundly declared; 'The Arab states stand by nature at the head of the peace-loving countries.' In the struggle for peace-not-war both Israel and the Arab League were strong competitors.

This struggle for peace may have been the declared aim: the reality was the terror raids of the fedayun which helped finally to destroy Ben Gurion's promise that there would be no aggressive war. 'Fedayun' means 'self-sacrificer', usually native Palestinians, disgruntled and desperate men, trained by Egypt to go forth from the Gaza Strip and revenge themselves on the Jews who had taken from them lands and nationality. Fedayun raiders attacked lonely farms, machine-gunned electric power stations and schools, and attacked isolated frontier posts.

To the Israeli, the fedayun was a marauder, a murderer stealing into a peaceful country, not itself using such tactics, and taking petty but hateful vengeance on any Israeli he met. To the Arab, he is a dedicated warrior, a Saladin in a twentieth century context. If no peace exists, it could be argued, any tactics are justified. Arab land is wrongfully occupied by non-Arabs. Arabs have been thrust out of their own country. To counter these injustices heroic men enter Israel to attack the foreigner in his fortress. Do these tactics differ in any important way from the tactics the Jews used against the British in the last years of the Mandate—or the methods of any European resistance?

Despite his romantic name, the fedayun was no unpaid volunteer, dedicating himself to battle against the usurper: he was a volunteer paid a handsome monthly salary. Not a soldier but an infiltrator, something between an intelligence agent committing sabotage and a free-lance guerilla.

The United Nations agency committed to maintaining peace on the frontier was the United Nations Truce Organisation, controlled by Lieut.-General Burns, a remarkable and impressively impartial Canadian. UNTSO, however, was largely concerned with border incidents; fedayun raids were outside its scope.

Israeli anger against the raiders, against murder and wanton destruction grew, directed against Egypt—their organiser, and the Gaza Strip—their source. In self-defence, the Israelis developed the theory of retaliation, a massive attack to create a deterrent. They did not look to the UN for protection but rather (in the words of Prime Minister Eshkol in the Arab–Israeli crisis of 1967), 'we rely on our own forces, and not on international forces.' On 28 February 1955, the Israelis mounted the Gaza Raid, a large scale retaliatory operation which was to have the immediate effect of transforming the whole situation in the Middle East. Israeli soldiers invaded the Gaza Strip at two separate points, attacked a military encampment, set fire to a military truck and killed its occupants. Twenty-six Egyptian soldiers were killed and two civilians. A new phase in Arab–Israeli relations had begun.

Before the Gaza Raid, despite the bellicose tone of Cairo Radio, President Nasser had privately assured Lieut.-General Burns that he had no wish for trouble on his Israel frontiers: in the changed atmosphere after the Raid he said he could no longer guarantee peace on his borders, no longer hold back men who might have lost brothers in the Raid. In political terms, this new attitude resulted in Egypt's search for arms, ending so dramatically with the Egypt–Czech arms deal.

In a public speech, Nasser described his search for arms, his appeals to England, France and America. All the Western Powers were prepared to let him have the armaments he needed but only on terms Nasser regarded as unacceptable to an independent Egypt. Only in Prague did he find men willing to sell arms on a strictly commercial basis. Nasser went on to underline this point by asserting that 'this commercial agreement does not open the way to Russian or foreign influence.' In Western eyes, Communist aircraft meant Russian influence: Russia had entered the Middle East again. From the Czech arms deal can be traced all the mounting suspicion in the West which led finally to complete breakdown.

3 · Tripartite (Britain, France and the United States) declaration on Security in the Arab – Israel Zone (June 1950)

The Governments of the United Kingdom, France, and the United States, having had occasion during the recent Foreign Ministers meeting in London to review certain questions affecting the peace and stability of the Arab states and Israel, and particularly that of the supply of arms and war material to these states, have resolved to make the following statements:

1. The three Governments recognised that the Arab states and Israel all need to maintain a certain level of armed forces for the purpose of assuring their internal security and their legitimate self-defence and to permit them to play their part in the defence of the area as a whole. All applications for arms or war materials for these countries will be considered in the light of these principles. In this connection the three Governments wish to recall and reaffirm the terms of the statements made by their representatives on the Security Council on 4 August 1949 in which they declared their opposition to the development of an arms race between the Arab states and Israel.

2. The three Governments declare that assurances have been received from all the states in question, to which they permit arms to be supplied from their countries, that the purchasing state does not intend to undertake any act of aggression against any other state. Similar assurances will be requested from any other state in the area to which they permit arms to be supplied in the future.

3. The three Governments take this opportunity of declaring their deep interest in and their desire to promote the establishment and maintenance of peace and stability in the area and their unalterable opposition to the use of force or threat of force between any of the states in that area. The three Governments, should they find that any of these states was preparing to violate frontiers or armistice lines, would, consistently with their obligations as members of the United Nations, immediately take action, both within and outside the United Nations, to prevent such violation.

4 · Extract from Statement by the Israel Prime Minister before the Knesset, 31 May 1950

The Knesset has surely noted that the three-power declaration is a unilateral instrument, issued to define the policy of the above powers towards the state of Israel and the Arab states on the question of arms and security. It is not necessary to stress here that the policy of the state of Israel is formulated only by the government of Israel.

Insofar as the declaration is designed to strengthen security and peace, even if only in the restricted Arab–Israel zone, it will receive the faithful support of the government of Israel. In the view of the government of Israel, the bolstering of peace in one corner of the world will contribute directly and indirectly, to bolstering peace throughout the world.

The government of Israel welcomes the statement of the three powers against an arms race between the Arab states and Israel.

This statement, as it is noted in the declaration, was made by the three powers in the Security Council as early as 4 August 1949. But the government of Israel must call attention, with astonishment and concern, to the fact that from that time to the present, as before the above date, the furnishing of arms has continued to one side only—the Arab states, which have not ceased to threaten a new war against Israel and up to the present have refused to discuss peace with us. At the same time there is a constant refusal to furnish arms and war material to Israel. This discrimination undermines the security of the state of Israel and endangers the peace in the Near East.

The three powers now inform us that they have received assurances from the states to which arms have been supplied that they harbour no aggressive designs on any other state. But these assurances by the Arab states have not been accompanied by any practical guarantee. Moreover they patently contradict the ceaseless preparations for war against the state of Israel.

Whoever knows the truth of the situation in the Arab lands will understand without hesitation that the arms set to these states, if used at all, will be used against Israel, and perhaps against Israel alone.

The government of Israel expresses satisfaction that the three powers now recognise that Israel has no less a need than the Arab states to maintain armed forces of a certain level.

Israel has never had, and never will have, aggressive intentions against anyone. Israel's hand is extended in peace to all the Arab states, severally and jointly. But Israel has the right and the duty to look after its own security, and the three powers have recognised this. The government of Israel hopes that this recognition will be translated into action, and that the discrimination against Israel in the supply of arms will be stopped completely by the governments that have signed the declaration.

The government of Israel received with particular satisfaction the public announcement by the three powers of their deep interest in and their desire to promote peace and stability in the Arab states and Israel, and of their unalterable opposition to the use of force or threat of the use of force by any state in this part of the world.

The three powers have pledged to take action against every violation of the frontiers or armistice lines, in accordance with their obligations as members of the United Nations. This pledge applies equally to the frontiers of the Arab states and to the domain of Israel, as fixed in armistice agreements with Egypt, Transjordan, Syria and Lebanon.

As a government directly concerned and as a member of the United Nations, the government of Israel feels obliged to state that it is not sufficient merely to prevent hostilities among neighbours. There is also a need to support and accelerate the negotiations for an enduring peace among all nations, among them Israel and the Arab states, and for this purpose it is essential to employ the full authority and resources of the United Nations.

The government of Israel will lend its hand faithfully to any endeavour designed to strengthen peace among all nations, and to raise the power and authority of the United Nations.

5 · Statement by the Arab League Council, 21 June 1950

The government of the Arab states, severally and jointly, have studied the joint declaration issued by the United Kingdom, France and the United States on 25 May 1950.

The Arab states have agreed to issue the following statement:

1. No-one is more anxious than the Arab states about the preservation of peace and stability in the Middle East. The Arab lands stand by nature at the head of the peace-loving countries. Successive events have proved the degree of their respect for the United Nations Charter.

2. If the Arab states have shown, and continue to show, an interest in meeting their military needs, this has been due to their deep sense of responsibility for safeguarding the internal security of their countries, insuring the legitimate defence of their neutrality and fulfilling the obligation of safeguarding international security in this region. This is primarily the obligation of the Arab states and of the Arab League as a regional organisation under Article 52 of the United Nations Charter.

3. Even before the three powers ever thought of issuing their declaration, the Arab governments on their own initiative had decided to express the peaceful intentions of the Arabs and to refute the allegations that Israel has persisted in circulating to the effect that the Arab states are requesting arms for aggressive purposes. The Arab states hereby reiterate their peaceful intentions and declare that the arms that have been, or may be, ordered from the three powers or from others will be used solely for defensive purposes.

4. It goes without saying that the level of armed forces maintained by every state for defence purposes and for participation in the maintenance of international security is a matter that can only be estimated by the state concerned. It is also subject to various factors, chiefly the size of the population, the area of the country and the length and diversity of its frontiers.

5. The Arab states take note of the assurances that they have received to the effect that the three powers did not intend by their declaration to favour Israel, or to exert pressure on the Arab states to enter into negotiations with Israel, or to affect the final settlement of the Palestine problem or to preserve the *status quo*; but that they did intend to express their opposition to the use of force or to the violation of the armistice lines.

6. The Arab states declare that the most preferable and reliable measures for maintaining peace and stability in the Middle East would consist in solving its problems on the basis of right and justice, re-establishing the conditions of understanding and harmony that once prevailed and hastening the execution of the United Nations resolution on the return of the Palestine refugees to their homes and on compensation for their material losses.

7. The Arab states also take note of assurances given them that the three-power declaration, both in its manner of presentation and in its provision for prior guarantees from the states purchasing arms, neither signifies the division of this region into zones of influence nor in any way infringes on the independence and sovereignty of the Arab states.

8. It is self-evident that the doubts, which the assurances mentioned in the preceding paragraph were designed to dispel, were raised by paragraph 3 of the three-power declaration which laid down that, if the three powers should find that any state of this region was preparing to violate the frontiers or armistice lines of another state, they would immediately take action, within or outside the United Nations, to prevent such violation.

There is no doubt that action alone will dispel these doubts, if it demonstrates that the three powers are in fact concerned with maintaining peace in the Middle East impartially and on the basis of right and justice and respect for the sovereignty of the states and without subjecting them to domination or influence.

9. In conclusion the Arab states can only affirm once again that, despite their anxiety for peace, they cannot approve any action that would harm their sovereignty and their independence.

6 · Nasser's announcement of the Egyptian agreement with Czechoslovakia for the purchase of arms (extract) 27 September 1955

My Brothers,

I am glad to speak to you today for I now recall my last talk to the men of the armed forces some months ago. I remember also that I spoke then to thousands of officers. Now I see them amongst us. I see them carrying out their duty on the frontiers of our homeland for the safety of our country and for the glory of our country.

When I speak to you now, my brothers, I speak to all the men of the armed forces: I speak to all the men of the fatherland; I speak to Egypt—Egypt which revolted on 23 July 1952—Egypt which placed its faith in the goals of this Revolution; Egypt which was determined to achieve these goals—Egypt which finally threw off the occupation and threw off slavery. When I speak to you today, I speak to all Egypt.

The fifth goal of your Revolution was to set up a strong national army. From the beginning of the Revolution you have all exerted every effort to achieve this goal and we have worked with you with all our might and with every means at our disposal. We have worked with you to achieve this goal because to achieve it means liberty: to achieve it means glory; to achieve it means dignity.

My brothers, we met the greatest obstacles—we met many difficulties in achieving our aim. We did everything we could to set up military factories; we did everything we could to provide the army with the heavy armaments it needed; and we did everything we could so that Egypt's army might be a strong national army.

Yes, my brothers we did a lot.

But there were the greatest difficulties in our way. We believed that if we wanted to create such an army for Egypt we had to preserve our freedom. We believed that if we wanted to achieve this strong national army for Egypt, we had to become free in our internal and our foreign policies.

My brothers, we will never agree that this army be formed at the expense of this country's freedom, or at the expense of this country's glory, or at the expense of this country's dignity. We have always been determined that the formation of this strong national army should go hand in hand with true liberty and real glory.

We have proclaimed Egypt's policy on many occasions. We declared that Egypt after the Revolution of July 23 would go forward with its independent policy; it would go forward having rid itself of imperialism; it would go forward having rid itself of domination; and it would go forward having rid itself of foreign influence. These were our hopes and these were your hopes. We did everything we could to preserve these hopes. We did everything we could, my brothers, to preserve these goals—and we were confronted by many obstacles.

You know that heavy weapons are controlled by the big powers. You know that the big powers have never agreed to supply our army with heavy weapons except with conditions and except with stipulations. You know that we refused these conditions and these stipulations because we are jealous of our true freedom and we are jealous of our independent policy. We are anxious that Egypt have a strong independent policy so that we may make of Egypt a new independent personality which will really rid itself of imperialism, will really rid itself of occupation, will really rid itself of foreign domination in all its aspects. We have been making progress along this path.

Today, my brothers, we hear an outcry from London, we hear an outcry from Washington about the arming of Egypt's troops. But I would like to tell you that throughout the last three years we have tried to get heavy weapons for the army by every means, not for aggressive purposes, not to attack, not to make war, but for defence, for security, for peace.

We wanted to strengthen our army so as to provide security for ourselves, to provide security for our nation, to provide security for our 'Arabism'. We wanted to get weapons for the army so that we could always feel secure, safe, and tranquil. We never intended to strengthen our army for aggressive purposes. We never intended to strengthen our army for wars. We do not want arms for aggression. We want arms so that we can be tranquil, so that we feel at peace and not threatened.

On this occasion I would like to tell you, my brothers, the story of the arming of our troops. When the Revolution took place we went to each of the states, we went to every quarter to get weapons for the army. We went to Britain; we went to France; we went to America; we went to the rest of the states to get weapons for the army in the interest of peace and defence. What did we get? We got only demands. They wanted to arm the troops after we had signed a document or after we had signed a pact. We declared that even though we had wanted and had decided to arm our troops, we would never sign a document.

We requested arms but what was the result? The result, my brothers, is a long and bitter story. I remember now, I remember as I talked to you that we sometimes humiliated ourselves but we never abandoned our principles. We humiliated ourselves when we requested arms—we begged for arms—but at the same time we were determined to hold to our principles and we were determind to preserve our high ideals. And what was the result? Never, my brothers, could we achieve our goal, the greatest goal for which the Revolution was undertaken, the creation of a strong national army.

France always bargained with us. She bargained with us over North Africa. She says to us, 'We will give you arms on the condition that you should not criticise our position in North Africa, and on condition that you relinquish your "Arabism", that you relinquish your humanitarianism and on condition that you should keep silent and close your eyes when you see the massacres in North Africa.'

We said to her, 'How can we relinquish our "Arabism"? How can we give up our humanitarianism? We never can.'

Now I'll tell you the story of America. From the time of the Revolution we asked for arms and we were promised arms. And what was the result?

The promise was a promise circumscribed with conditions. We would get arms if we signed a mutual security pact. We would get arms if we would sign some form of alliance. We refused to sign a mutual security pact. We refused to sign any form of alliance. And, my brothers, we could never get a single weapon from America.

What was the story of England? England told us that she was ready to supply us arms. We accepted gratefully. What was the result? England provided us with a quantity of arms which was not sufficient to achieve the goals of this Revolution.

What was the result of all this, my brothers? The army opposing us is obtaining arms from various parts of the world. Israel's army has been able to obtain arms from England, France, Belgium, Canada, Italy and from various other states. It can always find someone to supply it arms, while we read in the foreign press—in the British, American or French newspapers—that Israel's army can defeat all the Arab armies combined. It was only last month, my brothers, that I read many articles in that sense, that the Israeli army could defeat Egypt, that the Israeli army could beat the Arabs, that the Israeli army was superior in armament, that the Israeli army was superior in equipment.

This is what they have said in their press and I said to them, since you feel like this why do you prevent us from obtaining arms? I asked them this, and what was the result? France complained about our feelings towards North Africa, and prevented us from obtaining arms.

When we saw this, when we saw this domination, when we saw this influence which was being used against us, we decided to ask all the states of the world to supply us arms without conditions. I told them these arms would not be used for aggression, that they would be used for defence.

I said this, my brothers, in the name of Egypt to America, to England, to France, to Russia, to Czechoslavakia and to the rest of the states and I waited for their answers. I waited, and what was the result? I got answers from some of them that I could get arms with conditions. I refused, for I have already told you that although we are ready to humiliate ourselves by asking for arms, we will never abandon our principles.

We received a reply from Czechoslovakia saying that she was prepared to supply arms in accordance with our needs and those of Egypt's army on a commercial basis, the transaction to be considered like any other commercial transaction. We agreed and last week Egypt signed a commercial agreement with Czechoslovakia to supply us arms. This agreement permits Egypt to pay in Egyptian products such as cotton and rice. This offer we gratefully accepted.

Today, my brothers, as I talk to you I sense the outcry raised here and there—an outcry in London, and outcry in Washington. These outcries seek to continue to control us, to continue to influence us.

We will fight to destroy this control. We will fight to destroy this influence.

When I hear someone say that this opens the way for Russian influence or foreign influence in Egypt or the Middle East, I think of the remote past, and I say that this commercial agreement without conditions does not open the way for Russian or foreign influence, but, my brothers, it means the eradication of the foreign influence which so long oppressed us and dominated us.

My brothers, when we are able to equip our army with the necessary arms without conditions or restrictions, we destroy foreign control—that control which I have felt and which you have felt in the guise of equipping our army and in the guise of providing it with arms. Those who talk to us about foreign influence know that they themselves have no intention of seeing foreign influence wiped out.

We intend to destroy foreign influence. Egypt—independent Egypt, revolutionary Egypt, strong Egypt—will never allow foreign influence in her land. They know we will never accept their influence, and their control. They know that Egypt after the Revolution of 23 July has determined to destroy forever foreign influence, foreign oppression and foreign control and to go forward as a free independent power with her own foreign policy, motivated by her own interests and not by the interest of any of the foreign camps.

They know this when they talk of influence for they think that it is their influence which has come to an end in this country—that it is their influence which has gone away forever.

Today we are a free and independent nation. We will fight for our liberty and we will fight for our independence and may God be with us all.

7 · Extract from statement on foreign affairs by Israel Premier and Foreign Minister, Moshe Sharett, 18 October 1955

Renewed Egyptian Aggression The renewal of Egyptian aggressive actions along the Gaza strip jeopardised the security of our settlements in that border area and deeper in the country. The Egyptians resorted to the odious tactic of sending gangs deep into Israel to commit acts of murder and destruction. Vigorous reaction became imperative and the Defence Army of Israel struck against one of the nests of the gangsters. With the cessation, however, of attacks in the south, similar gangs began to operate in the northern sections of the country.

If Egypt proposes once more to disregard the obligations it has recently undertaken, we reserve to ourselves the freedom to act in accordance with the requirements of the situation.

A most conspicuous violation of the Armistice Agreements is implicit in the recent Egyptian regulations regarding entry into the Gulf of Eilat (Aqaba) aimed at obstructing the passage of Israel ships to the southern harbour of our country. These regulations are in contravention not only of the Armistice Agreements, but of resolutions of the Security Council and of principles of international law relating to the freedom of shipping in open waters and in straits between seas. Here, too, we reserve for ourselves full freedom of action at the time and in the manner we shall find suitable.

Egypt–Czechoslovak Arms Deal And now, honoured members of the Knesset, I come to the very serious event which occurred some three weeks ago and which has cast a deep shadow on the entire scene of the State's foreign and defence affairs. I refer to the agreement between the ruler of Egypt and the Czechoslovak Government—which from a political and military standpoint implies the linking up between Egypt and the entire Soviet Bloc—for the supply of heavy and modern arms to Egypt, by all accounts in very considerable quantities.

This departure is liable to bring about a revolutionary and ominous change in Israel's security situation.

Both parties attempted to describe the arrangement as a purely commercial deal—perfectly simple and legitimate. Both parties went on to explain that the arms were merely intended to satisfy the defence needs of a free and sovereign state. Neither of the parties ignored Israel or pretended that the arms were not destined to be used against her.

Both sought to justify this great addition to Egyptian arms with the argument that they were to enable a handicapped Egypt to attain to Israel's level of armament.

Egypt's 'Dedication to Peace'

Here is his [Nasser's] pledge of dedication to peace as made in a statement to an Egyptian paper:

'It is utterly inconceivable that Egypt should ever consider peace with Israel or even think of recognising it'

And in another statement:

'The problem of Palestine will not be solved and there will be no peace between us and the Jews so long as even the slightest right of the Arabs of that country is controlled by the enemy. A man can forget everything except blood, vengeance and honour'

And in another paper:

'The Arabs consider Israel an artificial state which has to be annihilated'

And in one of his speeches:

'Israel is a sword suspended over us, over our freedom and honour. Never will we negotiate with Israel'

Yet another clarion call from the same bugle:

'We cannot but be in a state of war with Israel. This impels us to mobilise all Arab resources for its final liquidation. We ask that our production should be military production and meet our war needs. We want all our newspapers and radio stations to proclaim the total mobilisation of forces for the liberation of Palestine.'

Widening Gap

Since the establishment of the State we have been under the threat of the widening gap between the military power of the Arab states and that of our own army—which also is growing, which improves consistently, which progresses in equipment and fighting capacity, but which necessarily lags behind quantitatively as regards both manpower and weapons.

That is why our cry has always been: No arms race. No supply of any weapons whatever to states which maintain war, which plot war, which flatly refuse to make peace. And something in this direction has been achieved.

The supply of arms by Czechoslovakia to Egypt is dangerous because it flows to an Egypt which is hostile to us. The same applies to the American arms which are at present being supplied to Iraq or to arms of any power which may at any future time be supplied to Syria. These countries are hostile towards us and their arms are liable to be used against us. It is our position that arms must not be given or sold to states which do not seek peace states whose declared and real policies are war.

Thus it is our stand that there is a duty and an obligation to sell or grant arms to that state which offers peace—but which is compelled to defend itself as against neighbours who deny it peace and conspire aggression against it.

Security Pact

However, not only arms are needed by us. The change which has taken place in these weeks and which is pregnant with grave implications has invested with additional urgency Israel's need for a security pact—not for one dependent on a parallel agreement with Egypt, but a defence agreement made with Israel to meet the strengthening of the offensive potential of Egypt.

The defence pact which we need is not directed and cannot be directed at aggression against any other power. It is designed to serve as one of the basic pillars of our defence against aggression. Therefore, such a pact is justified and vital. It can be justified to every power which is in a position to conclude such an agreement, and yet would withhold lest it complicates its position in relation to states. It can be like-wise justified to any power that is liable to stigmatise it on the false pretence that it is aimed against her.

But just as I have emphasised our need for a security pact in addition to the supply of arms, I must stress even more emphatically that no security pact is a substitute for arms. With all the importance attaching to a security pact with the United States (and who knows whether it will materialise), not in this alone lies our salvation.

At this hour, from this House, from this our Capital, let the call go out to all Israel citizens, to the Jewish people in its dispersion and to the whole world—arms for Israel.

8 · The Fedayun raids

From the Chief of Egyptian Army Intelligence in the Gaza Strip, Colonel Mustafa Hafez to the Governor of the Strip

To the Administrative Governor-General;

1. The above-mentioned Yunes Mabrak is a representative of our office and one of the most faithful; he is a man who can be entrusted with important and dangerous missions. He was an example of heroism and supreme courage in his dedication and readiness for self-sacrifice on behalf of Egypt and the Egyptian armed forces.

2. The above-mentioned volunteered for the Palestinian fedayun forces and, infiltrating into Israel, carried out with his comrades acts of sabotage, dynamiting and killing. The following are some of his actions which are worthy of praise:

A On 29 August 1955 he carried out the following deeds:

- i) Killed three workers in an orange-grove at Bet Hanun
- ii) Murdered a mechanic in the electric power station near Al Kabeiba
- iii) Blew up the main pylon of the 'Voice of Israel Overseas' radio station
- iv) Attacked the farm settlement of Juala near Zarnoga in the vicinity of Al Kabeiba, in which one man was killed, four wounded, one building was destroyed and damage inflicted on the village co-operative store.
- v) Ambushed a convoy of vehicles.

B On 30 August 1955 he carried out the following deeds:

- i) Ambushed a vehicle near the village of Ajur and killed three people. The vehicle was destroyed.
- ii) Attacked the village of Tzumeil and blew up one of the buildings.
- iii) Ambushed a vehicle on the Plugot-Bet Govrin road.
- iv) At the same site, he ambushed three army vehicles.

3. Since the above-mentioned is one of the accused in the murder trial No. 26/55, and taking into account his wonderful deeds, we request that merciful consideration and appreciation be given to his past record of sacrificial actions so that a way may be found to help him as far as possible. It will also be possible to use him in the future if he sees that the authorities appreciate the results of his courageous deeds.

We therefore request that you deal compassionately with our representative and that you close the file against him.

Mustafa Hafez
Commander, Palestine Intelligence

9 · The Arab case against Israel

The remmants of Palestine's Arabs who have continued to live in the Zionist settler-state since 1948 have their own 'Bantustans', 'their native reserves', their 'Ghettoes'—although the institution which they encounter in their daily lives is given by the Zionist authorities the euphemistic name, 'security zone'.

About 90 per cent of the Arabs living under Israel's jurisdiction live in such 'security zones'.

Alone in the Zionist settler-state, these Arabs live under *martial law*. Whereas, in other parts of the country, civil administration prevails, in the Arab-inhabited 'security zones' the administrative functionaries are military officers, serving under the Ministry of Defence. Arabs charged with offences under the martial law in force in the 'security zones' (the 'Emergency [Defence] Regulations') are prosecuted before military tribunals, the decisions of which are not appealable. Deportation and forced residence, by fiat of the Military Governor, are commonplace.

Alone in the Zionist settler-state, Arab inhabitants of the 'security zones' are subject to the *pass system*, which harshly restricts their movement and travel.

Alone in the Zionist settler-state, Arabs are denied the basic rights of expression, assembly, and association. They are not permitted to publish newspapers or to form political organisations.

Educational opportunities for Arabs are severely restricted; the higher the level of education, the more discriminatory the restriction of opportunities. Nor is the quality of the educational system to which Arabs have disproportionately-limited access faintly comparable to the educational system open to Jews.

Economically, Arabs in the Zionist settler-state suffer from a threefold handicap: their limited access to employment opportunities creates large-scale unemployment; such employment as they are permitted to obtain is confined largely to menial services; and they are denied the right to 'equal pay for equal work'.

The agricultural lands and homes of the Arabs of the Zionist settler-state are subject to confiscation by administrative decree, under a succession of drastic laws, introduced by the state between 1948 and 1953, which deny aggrieved owners the ability to seek redress through the courts. Whole Arab villages have been expropriated and given to Jews for the establishment of Zionist settlements.

Arab participation in the administration of the Zionist settler-state, on any level of meaningful responsibility, is virtually unknown; in most government departments, Arab participation *on any level* is completely non-existent. Even in the government office charged with Arab affairs, no Arab is employed!

Finally, the enjoyment by Arabs of the elementary right to citizenship in their own country is curtailed by *statutory discrimination*. Whereas a Jew, under the Nationality Law, is eligible for citizenship immediately upon arrival, indigenous Arabs of the Zionist settler-state are subject to a system of qualified eligibility which has left a majority of Israel's Arabs languishing in the limbo of non-citizenship.

3 · The High Dam Loan and its consequences

Importance of the High Dam

To President Nasser the construction of the High Dam was of major political importance: he had staked his political career on negotiating a loan for the building of the Dam. To Egypt the Dam meant more cultivated land to feed her rising population.

Egypt's population was increasing by 2.6 per cent a year. The High Dam would produce an increase in the cultivated area of 25 per cent barely sufficient to keep abreast of the population expansion. What the Egyptian government hoped for too was an overall stimulus to the Egyptian economy, by increasing the number of skilled workers and by providing a cheap source of electric power. With a stroke of luck the Egyptian economy might in fact reach the point of economic take-off by the impetus provided by the work involved in the actual building of the Dam as well as by the facilities the completed Dam would provide.

To Egypt the Dam was vital and the money for its construction was to come initially from the World Bank where American influence was paramount. Israeli–Arab relations put this loan out of court. The Gaza Raid (17 February 1955), Egypt's arms deal with Czechoslovakia quickened American suspicion that Egypt was increasingly coming under Soviet influence and negotiations were broken off. Personally and politically slighted by the peremptory attitude of the American Secretary of State, John Foster Dulles, Nasser looked elsewhere for funds, a search which led to the nationalisation of the Canal and subsequently to a Russian loan.

10 · The Egyptian approach to the World Bank, 17 December 1955

Mr Abdel Moneim El Kaissouni, Egyptian Minister of Finance, met yesterday with Acting Secretary of State Herbert Hoover, Jr., British Ambassador Sir Roger Makins and World Bank President Eugene Black for final talks before his departure for Cairo.

During their stay in Washington, Mr Kaissouni and his colleagues have been carrying on discussions with the management of the World Bank and representatives of the United States and United Kingdom Governments concerning possible assistance in the execution of the High Aswan Dam project.

The United States and British Government assured the Egyptian Government through Mr Kaissouni of their support in this project, which would be of inestimable importance in the development of the Egyptian economy and in the improvement of welfare of the Egyptian people. Such assistance would take the form of grants from the United States and the United Kingdom toward defraying foreign exchange costs of the first stages of the work. This phase, involving the Coffer Dam, foundations for the main dam, and auxiliary work will take from four to five years. Further, assurance has been given to Mr Kaissouni that the Governments of the United States and the United Kingdom would, subject to legislative authority, be prepared to consider synpathetically in the light of the then existing circumstances further support toward financing the later stages to supplement World Bank financing.

Mr Kaissouni plans to leave Washington for Egypt today and it is understood that he will report to his Government on his talks here. Final understandings with the British and American Governments and the World Bank will await Mr Kaissouni's consultation with the Egyptian Government.

11 · America's decision to withdraw her support for the High Dam, 19 July 1956

At the request of the Government of Egypt, the United States joined in December 1955 with the United Kingdom and with the World Bank in an offer to assist Egypt in the construction of a high dam on the Nile at Aswan. This project is one of great magnitude. It would require an estimated 12 to 16 years to complete at a total cost estimated at some 1,300,000,000 dollars, of which over 900,000,000 represents local currency requirements. It involves not merely the rights and interests of Egypt but of other states whose waters are contributory, including Sudan, Ethiopia, and Uganda.

The December offer contemplated an extension by the United States and United Kingdom of grant aid to help finance certain early phases of the work, the effects of which would be confined solely to Egypt, with the understanding that accomplishment of the project as a whole would require a satisfactory resolution of the question of Nile water rights. Another important consideration bearing upon the feasibility of the undertaking, and thus the practicability of American aid, was Egyptian readiness and ability to concentrate its economic resources upon this vast construction program.

Developments within the succeeding seven months have not been favorable to the success of the projects, and the US Government has concluded that it is not feasible in present circumstances to participate in the project. Agreement by the riparian states has not been achieved, and the ability of Egypt to devote adequate resources to assure the project's success has become more uncertain than at the time the offer was made.

This decision in no way reflects or involves any alteration in the friendly relations of the Government and people of the United States toward the Government and people of Egypt.

The United States remains deeply interested in the welfare of the Egyptian people and in the development of the Nile. It is prepared to consider at an appropriate time and at the request of the riparian states what steps might be taken toward a more effective utilization of the water resources of the Nile for the benefit of the peoples of the region. Furthermore, the United States remains ready to assist Egypt in its effort to improve the economic conditions of its people and is prepared, through its appropriate agencies, to discuss these matters within the context of funds appropriated by the Congress.

12 · John Foster Dulles' refusal of the loan for the High Dam

Still unsure of his and America's decision, about 16 July Dulles discussed the issue cursorily with President Eisenhower. He informed the President of the reasons for deciding as he himself, Dulles, should consider wise. The President did not, for his part, positively order the Secretary to withhold the loan. He was annoyed he said, because, while he was working for peace in the Middle East, Nasser was acquiring arms that might be used against Israel. Where, then, was the point of finding money for the Dam? If the Secretary should come down on that side, then he would concur in the denial of the loan.

Two days later, the British Ambassador, Sir Roger Makins, was called to the State Department: the British were in partnership in the proposed loan for the Dam, and both had an interest, each for itself, in the Middle East in general. Dulles informed Makins that he was dubious about making the loan, not that he was definitely about to refuse it. Sir Roger urged the Secretary to consider his ultimate decision with utmost care. Dulles then asked Sir Roger to consult Eden about it, because the Egyptian Ambassador was coming in the following day, that is 19 July. Dulles exploited his trouble with the Senate as a means of spurring the Ambassador and Eden on to agree with him to drop the loan. He pressed Makins with a plea that he, Dulles, must avoid the Senate rider hindering the loan. He pleaded that he was under intolerable pressure and time was of the essence. Makins, as already said, replied that the tactics would have to be 'playing it long'. London was as embarrassed as Dulles to learn that Nasser now positively wanted the loan, and that his Ambassador was on the way to get it, for they also had reason to be chagrined by Nasser's recent acts of arrogance. But they knew that Nasser was violent in temper and unreliable in his reactions. They also counselled, 'Play it long'. When Sir Roger consulted London, he came back with further express words of caution from Eden and Selwyn Lloyd, the British Foreign Secretary. Their opinion was 'We leave the decision to your (Dulles's) judgement whether you grant or rescind the offer of the loan. But we do not wish you to be precipitate; we wish you to play it long.' The tactics of delay were then the tactics agreed upon by the United States and Britain, in preference to any unceremonious refusal of the loan. Eden and Selwyn Lloyd had begged Dulles not to act, to use diplomatic classical language, brusque, that is to say, abruptly-cum-roughly.

Only a couple of days previously the French Ambassador in Washington, Couve de Murville, had given the State Department a serious warning. He said in so many words, 'To deny the loan for the Aswan Dam to Nasser is a very dangerous action; it can affect the Suez Canal. I know Nasser: as you know, I was Ambassador for my government in Cairo, for several years. Beware how you handle the situation with the loan, because a most likely consequence of a refusal is the seizure of the Suez Canal'. The warning was laughed at by officials. It should not have been, for another reason altogether: Egyptian politicians had for decades been jealous of the Suez Canal Company's status and it was a favourite subject of attack, juridically and politically.

On 19 July 1956, Dulles was in the office at work, as usual, at shortly after 8.00 am. He repeated his consultation with the President, the issue not closed. At about 11.00 his phone rang and he was told that Ambassador Hussein was on his way up to the office. Two very high State Department career officials were present in the room with Dulles. The Ambassador entered with his aide. He himself was a not unwelcome figure. He had held his position since long before Nasser's deposition of Naguib and, according to some State Department officials, was not an idolator of Nasser. Indeed, he was said to be rather inclined towards the Western point of view in the struggle for mastery in the Middle East and in the world in general. Dulles did not dislike him personally.

Dulles began to explain the many difficulties he was encountering in clinching the loan. This took him a little time, as he always spoke very carefully, in rather pedantic language and syntax.

The Ambassador began to advance questions on certain matters. The Aswan Dam scheme, if it was to be helped, was, as the Ambassador had long known, to follow on an agreement between Egypt and the Sudan whereby Sudan's share of the upper waters of the Nile would be assigned satisfactorily to that country. But this had not yet been concluded, he was anxious about this. Dulles in each case put the other point of view. It seemed that Hussein, by the proper demeanour and rhetoric, might have an indefinite postponement or an alibi, rather than a complete refusal.

Then, as Dulles appeared to be bringing the various reasons against the loan to a head, all in tones rather sad and firm, the Ambassador became excited. He was sitting on the divan near the coffee table, while Dulles was sitting just on the other side of that same table in an armchair with his legs stretched out onto the table. At a certain point, Ambassador Hussein, perhaps remembering the instructions received in Cairo, became worried and agitated. He leaned forward over the table, gesticulating. 'Don't please say', he blurted out, 'you are going to withdraw the offer, because. . . .' (and he pointed to his pocket) 'we have the Russian offer to finance the Dam right here in my pocket.'

No nerve was so raw in all of Dulles's sensitive composition as Russia. He at once retorted, 'Well, as you have the money already, you don't need any from us. My offer is withdrawn.'

13 · President Nasser's account of the negotiations with the Western Powers and the World Bank over the proposed loan, 26 July 1956

As I told you, in 1953 we drew up a plan for the development of production in order to increase the national income. We said that we should increase the national income speedily because every year we increase by half a million, that is we shall number 40,000,000 30 years hence. Our standard of living is hardly considered a standard of living and is rated as a low one. We therefore have two moves to make: to produce in order to raise the standard of living and to produce in order to create an income—namely to double our production. The increase in production will bring an increase to the national income.

The raising of the standard of living requires an increase in income. We began to think and found that the Nile waters are wasted each year. We said that we should be able to benefit from the Nile waters. Someone told us about the High Dam in 1952. It was discussed in 1953. This project has been in existence ever since 1924. It will increase our arable land by 1,500,000 feddans. It would come into being after ten years and would provide us with about

2,000,000,000 kilowatts. Therefore the project in fact yields an income and has an effect on the standard of living and on raising the national revenue.

We began to face the obstacle of finance. We do not have enough money to meet the cost of this project, amounting to about 1,000,000,000 dollars over a period of ten years. We contacted the World Bank in 1953. The Bank said that there were obstacles and conditions at our end which did not give rise to confidence.

Discussions took place in December in America between the US Government, a British representative and a World Bank representative. When these long and bitter talks ended, proposals were advanced by the World Bank. These proposals were in the form of a reply which the World Bank sent to me. The Bank said that it was prepared to participate in financing the High Dam to the tune of 200,000,000 dollars after five years, and that the 200,000,000 dollars would not be lent to me in a lump sum but in instalments, as I should choose, and that we would negotiate over each instalment. In this reply there were also conditions imposed on Egypt for her to obtain this loan from the World Bank. These stated that the World Bank would lend 200,000,000 dollars, if requested, in foreign currency. Financing by the Bank and contributions paid to it would depend on agreement regarding the terms of the loan. The terms of the loan would have to be negotiated from time to time and, of course, we might either agree or disagree. Then it said that the loan depended on the following conditions:

The Bank must be completely reassured that the required foreign currency, which would come out of British or American grants, was not withheld; in other words, the Bank tied itself to British and American grants. It said that it would lend us 200,000,000 dollars provided the British and Americans were pleased with us.

Then again: The Egyptian Government must not undertake any foreign loan. We must not borrow a single mill from anyone. Likewise we must not conclude payments agreements—we must not make an arms agreement with Russia for example, except with the approval of the World Bank, of course. The same applies to payments agreements in excess of the amounts agreed upon from time to time between the Egyptian Government and the Bank, so that the World Bank would always have full knowledge of Egypt's state of affairs. Egypt would have had to check with the World Bank before undertaking any commitment.

Well, how can we make any progress in these circumstances?

In June 1956—last month—it was decided that Mr Shepilov, Russian Foreign Minister, should visit Egypt. At the same time the Director of the World Bank said he wanted to come. We told him: You will be welcome. Talks were held between the Egyptian Government and Mr Shepilov, Foreign Minister of the Soviet Union. The Soviet Foreign Minister expressed his readiness to help Egypt in all fields in which she asked for assistance to the extent of granting long-term loans. He said that everything in which they co-operated would be without restrictions or condition: all we had to do was ask them.

The next day the Director of the World Bank came and visited me at home at 10 o'clock or a little later. He said he had come to emphasise that the World Bank still adhered to its promise and to the statement it had made in February. He added that the Bank was determined to finance this project and that he could say that the US and British Governments—with whom he was in contact—were also going to keep their promises.

That is what happened up to about 20 June last. Our Ambassador to the USA returned to Egypt. He saw Dulles before he came. He told me that they were anxious to finance the project and to continue to help but that they thought that we did not want their help. I told him: Yes, we want them to finance the project; we thought they did not want to do it, that was what we thought: you can go back and tell them we want to talk and negotiate to finance this project. Ahmed Hussein, our Ambassador in Washington, returned to his post with the aim of seeing Dulles and asking him to reply to the memoranda which we had sent and to inform us of his opinion in this respect. Two days later the US Government issued a press communiqué.

4 · Nationalisation and the Western Powers

Chronology of Events

26 July	Nasser nationalised the Suez Canal declaring that the income from the Canal would be used to build the High Dam.
2 August	Recall of some reservists by Britain.
18 August	First London Conference.
10 September	Visit of Guy Mollet, French Prime Minister and Christian Pineau, Foreign Minister, to London.
11 September	Suez Canal Company order European pilots home.
19 September	Second London Conference sets up Canal Users Association.
23 September	Suez dispute referred to Security Council by France and Britain.

14 · President Nasser's announcement of the nationalisation of the Suez Canal Campany, 26 July 1956

We have a complex as a result of de Lesseps, Cromer and political occupation by way of economic occupation. This is the picture I had in mind—the picture of de Lesseps when he arrived in Egypt. De Lesseps arrived in Egypt on 7 November 1854.

This is how the story goes. He arrived in Alexandria and began to work cautiously and craftily. On 30 November 1854 after getting in touch with the Khedive Mohammed Said, de Lesseps secured the Canal concession. The following were the prominent points in the concession: Whereas our friend, Mr Ferdinand de Lesseps, has drawn our attention to the benefits which Egypt will derive from linking the Mediterranean with the Red Sea by means of a shipping route, and informed us of the possibility of forming a company for this purpose with the aid of capitalists, we have accepted the idea submitted to us and accordingly have given special authorisation for the organisation and the management of a company to dig the Suez Canal and exploit it. This was in 1854. In 1856, exactly 100 years ago, a firman was issued establishing the company. Egypt took 44 per cent of the company's shares and assumed the obligation for them to de Lesseps. The de Lesseps company was a private company, which had nothing to do with Governments, domination or occupation; it had nothing to do with colonisation. De Lesseps told the Khedive: I am your friend; I have come with the desire to benefit you by building a canal for you between the seas.

The Suez Canal company was formed. Egypt participated in 44 per cent of its shares. Egypt undertook to provide, gratis, workers for digging the Canal. One hundred and twenty thousand workers died digging the Canal for nothing; they dug the canal with our lives, our skeletons, our bones and our blood.

The agreement of 22 February 1866 started the agreements. Article 16 said that since the International Company of the Suez Canal was an Egyptian company, it was subject to the laws and customs of the country. Has it really been subject to the laws and customs of the country? The result of what de Lesseps told the Khedive in 1856 and of the friendship and loans was pure occupation in 1882. Egypt borrowed for this purpose. What did she do? During the Ismail regime Egypt was compelled to sell her share of the 44 per cent. England immediately came forward to buy the 44 per cent—Egypt's share in the Suez Canal; to buy it for how much? for £4,000,000. Then Ismail surrendered the five per cent profits which he was getting to the company in return for the company's abandonment of certain concessions which he had given it. He was compelled, after England bought from him 44 per cent of the shares for £4,000,000 to pay it five per cent in return for the profits which he had surrendered; in other words, Britain got Egypt's 44 per cent of the shares for nothing.

The income of the Suez Canal in 1955 amounted to £35,000,000, the equivalent of 100,000,000 dollars. This is the income of the Egyptian company, the Suez Canal Company. In return for the 120,000 Egyptians who perished digging it and for the money spent on building it, we get £1,000,000 or 3,000,000 dollars.

The Suez Canal, sitting in Paris, is a usurping company. It usurped our concessions. When he came here de Lesseps acted in the same manner as do certain people who come to hold talks with me. Does history repeat itself? On the contrary. We shall build the High Dam and we shall gain our usurped rights. We shall build the High Dam as we desire. We are determined. The Canal company annually takes £35,000,000. Why shouldn't we take it ourselves? . . .

Thus today, when we build the High Dam, we are also building the dam of dignity, freedom and grandeur. We are eliminating the dams of humiliation, and servility. . . . We look back to the past only to put an end to its effects. Now, O citizens, as the rights revert to their owners, now that our rights in the Suez Canal have reverted to us after 100 years, we are building the real foundations of sovereignty and the real edifice of grandeur and dignity. The Suez Canal was a state within a state; it was an Egyptian limited company which depended on foreign plots and on imperialism and the supporters of imperialism. The Suez Canal was built for Egypt and for Egypt's interests but it was a source of exploitation and extortion.

As I told you a little while ago, it is no shame to be poor and to strive and build my country. What is shameful, however, is to suck blood. They sucked our blood, and extorted and stole our rights. Today as we retrieve these rights, I declare on behalf of the Egyptian people that we shall preserve these rights and cherish them. We shall protect these rights and give our lives and blood for them. We shall protect these rights because thereby we shall be making up for the past. As we build the edifice of grandeur, freedom and dignity we feel that it can never be built or become complete unless we demolish the facades of oppression, humiliation and degradation. The Suez Canal was one of the facades of oppression, extortion and humiliation. Today, O citizens the Suez Canal has been nationalised and this decree has in fact been published in the Official Gazette and has become law. Today, O citizens we declare that our property has been returned to us. The rights about which we were silent have been restored to us. Today, citizens, with the annual income of the Suez Canal amounting to £35,000,000—that is, 100,000,000 dollars a year, and 500,000,000 dollars in five years—we shall not look for the 70,000,000 dollars of American aid.

Today we greet the fifth year of the revolution and in the same way as Farouk left on 26 July 1952, the old Suez Canal Company also leaves on the same day. . . . We shall march forward as one people who have vowed to work and to proceed on a holy march of industrialising and construction—nay, as one people who are solidly united in opposition to treachery and aggression and to imperialism and the supporters and antics of imperialism.

At this moment as I talk to you some of your Egyptian brethren are proceeding to administer the canal company and to run its affairs. They are taking over the canal company at this very moment—the Egyptian canal company, not the foreign canal company. They have started to take over the canal company and its property and to control shipping in the canal—the canal which is situated in Egyptian territory, which goes through Egyptian territory which is part of Egypt and which is owned by Egypt. They are now carrying out this task so that we can make up for the past and build new edifices of grandeur and dignity. May the Almighty grant you success, and may the peace and blessing of God be upon you.

15 · Suez Canal Company nationalisation law, 26 July 1956

Article 1. The Suez Canal Company is nationalised. All money, rights and obligations of the company are transferred to the State. All organisations and committees now operating the company are dissolved. Shareholders and holders of constituent shares shall be compensated in accordance to the value of the shares on the Paris Stock Market on the day preceding the enforcement of this law.

Payment of compensation shall take place immediately the State receives all the assets and property of the nationalised company.

Article 2. The management of the Suez Canal traffic utility will be in the hands of an independent body enjoying juristic personality and attached to the Ministry of Commerce. The formation of said body and the amount of compensation to be paid to its members shall be determined by order of the President of the Republic. This body will be invested with all the powers necessary for the proper management of the utility.

Article 3. The money and property of the nationalised company in Egypt and abroad are frozen. Banks, organisations and individuals are prohibited from disposing of same in any manner except by order of board mentioned in Article 2.

Article 4. Said Board shall retain all the employees and workers of the nationalised company. They will continue performing their duties and none can leave his work or give it up in any manner or for any reason except with the permission of the Authority mentioned in Article 2.

Article 5. Any contravention of Article 3 is punishable with imprisonment and a fine equal to three times the value of the money in question. Every contravention of Article 4 shall be punishable with imprisonment in addition to denying the person concerned any right to compensation, pension or end of service gratuity.

Article 6. This decree shall be published in the Official Gazette and will have the force of law from the day it is published. The Minister of Commerce is empowered to issue the necessary executory orders.

This decree shall bear the seal of the State and be executed as one of its laws.

16 · The attitude of the House of Commons to nationalisation, 27 July 1956

Mr Gaitskell asked the Prime Minister whether he has any statement to make on the reported action of the Egyptian Government in regard to the Suez Canal.

The Prime Minister: Yes, Sir. The unilateral decision of the Egyptian Government to expropriate the Suez Canal Company, without notice and in breach of the Concession Agreements, affects the rights and interests of many nations. Her Majesty's Government are consulting other Governments immediately concerned, with regard to the serious situation thus created. The consultations will cover both the effect of this arbitrary action upon the operation of the Suez Canal and also the wider questions which it raises.

Mr Gaitskell: On this side of the House, we deeply deplore this high-handed and totally unjustifiable step by the Egyptian Government. Has the Prime Minister in mind to refer this matter to the Security Council? Has he yet come to a decision on that point? In view of the seizure of the property of the Suez Canal Company and the vague statement about future compensation, will he bear in mind the desirability of blocking the sterling balances of the Egyptian Government?

The Prime Minister: I am quite sure the right hon. Gentleman will understand if I say that I would not wish to make a direct answer to his last question beyond saying that what he has mentioned has been already in our minds. As regards the Security Council, I would rather not say what action the countries concerned—we are in consultation, naturally, now with them—would wish to take, whether in the Security Council, or immediate diplomatic action, or whatever it may be.

Mr Clement Davies: May I be allowed to say, on behalf of myself and my colleagues, that we associate ourselves with what has been said by the Leader of the Opposition about this deplorable action?

17 · Hugh Gaitskell's speech in the House of Commons (extract), 2 August 1956

Moreover, while I have not hesitated to express my disagreement with the Government in their policy in the past, I must make it abundantly plain that anything they have done or not done in no way excuses Colonel Nasser's action in seizing the Canal.

The Egyptian argument is perfectly clear. It is that this is an Egyptian company and that as the Government of Egypt they are perfectly entitled to nationalise any company they wish to nationalise, provided that they pay compensation; as regards the right of transit through the Canal they have given assurances that they regard it as necessary to observe the 1888 Convention. I should like to give my answers, as I see it, to that case put forward by the Egyptian Government.

First, so far as my hon. and right hon. Friends are concerned at any rate, we certainly do not say that the act of nationalisation in itself is wrong. Nor would we say that the act of nationalising a foreign-owned company was necessarily wrong, provided that the compensation was reasonable and fair.

The real objections, it seems to me, are three. In the first place, as the Prime Minister has rightly emphasised, this is not an ordinary Company, conducting ordinary activities. It is a Company controlling an international waterway of immense importance to the whole of the rest of the world. It is, therefore, bound to be a matter of international concern when it changes hands.

Now the ownership and control of the Company is to be transferred to a single Power, to the hands of one State controlling it and, therefore, in a position even more than before to decide how the Canal shall be run. It may be said there is no need for anxiety because we have had these assurances about the 1888 Convention I am bound to say that it seems to me the strongest reason for having doubts in our minds as to whether we can accept these assurances has been the behavior of the Egyptian Government in stopping Israeli ships from going through, and equally important—indeed, even more important—the clear defiance of the Resolution of the United Nations condemning this action, passed in September 1951.

The second reason why I think we must take strong exception to this is that any confidence we might have had in an action of this kind was profoundly shaken by the manner in which it was carried out. It was done suddenly, without negotiation, without discussion, by force, and it was done on the excuse that this was the way to finance the Aswan Dam project. Colonel Nasser himself, at the conclusion of his speech[1] a week ago, said:

Thus, you will see that our wealth has been restored to us and that we shall not look forward to the Anglo-American financial aid amounting to 75 million dollars because we shall henceforth get from the profits of the Suez Canal the sum of 100 million dollars every year and in five years we shall secure 500 million dollars.

That, in effect, means that he is proposing to take the whole of the gross revenues of the Canal—almost all of them transit dues—and divert them for the purpose of the Aswan Dam. Yet he has promised compensation. How can he at one and the same time both keep the Canal going, spend the necessary money on the repairs, extensions and reconstruction, pay the compensation or service the compensation loan to the shareholders, and also find money for the Aswan Dam?

I do not think one can deny that this action is, first, to some extent a threat to access to the Canal in the light of what the Egyptians have done about the Israeli ships; secondly a warning that he may not maintain the Canal adequately; and, thirdly a very definite inplication that higher charges will be levied. As the Prime Minister has said, this is serious not only for us but for every maritime nation in the world; East and West, all are involved.

[1]see page 33

My third reason for thinking that we must object to this is that we cannot ignore—and this is a matter that the Prime Minister did not touch upon, no doubt for good reasons—the political background and the repercussions of the whole of this episode in the Middle East. We cannot forget that Colonel Nasser has repeatedly boasted of his intention to create an Arab empire from the Atlantic to the Persian Gulf. The French Prime Minister, M. Mollet, the other day quoted a speech of Colonel Nasser's and rightly said that it could remind us only of one thing—of the speeches of Hitler before the war.

Colonel Nasser has certainly made a number of inflammatory speeches against us and his Government has continually attempted subversion in Jordan and other Arab states; he has persistently threatened the State of Israel and made it plain from time to time that it is his purpose and intention to destroy Israel if he possibly can. That, if ever there was one, is a clear enough notice of aggression to come.

The fact is that this episode must be recognised as part of the struggle for the mastery of the Middle East. That is something which I do not feel that we can ignore. One may ask, 'Why does it involve the rest of the Middle East?' It is because of the prestige issues which are involved here. I said something about prestige when I spoke in the Middle East debate some months ago, and I must refer to it now, because prestige has quite considerable effects. If Colonel Nasser's prestige is put up sufficiently and ours is put down sufficiently, the effects of that in that part of the world will be that our friends desert us because they think we are lost, and go over to Egypt.

I have no doubt myself that the reason why Colonel Nasser acted in the way that he did, aggressively, brusquely, suddenly, was precisely because he wanted to raise his prestige in the rest of the Middle East. He wanted to show the rest of the Arab world—'See what I can do'. He wanted to challenge the West and to win.

It is all very familiar. It is exactly the same that we encountered from Mussolini and Hitler, in those years before the war. We must not underestimate the danger of the effect which this may have on the other Arab states.

Last of all, I come to a matter which cannot be ignored, at this moment just before the Recess. There has been much talk in the Press about the use of force in these circumstances. First, I would say that we need to be very careful what we say on this subject. It is unwise to discuss hypothetical situations in present conditions. Obviously, there are circumstances in which we might be compelled to use force, in self-defence or as a part of some collective defence measures. I do not myself object to the precautionary steps announced by the Prime Minister today; I think that any Government would have to do that, as we had to do it during the Persian crisis.

I must, however, remind the House that we are members of the United Nations, that we are signatories to the United Nations Charter, and that for many years in British policy we have steadfastly avoided any international action which would be in breach of international law or, indeed, contrary to the public opinion of the world. We must not, therefore, allow ourselves to get into a position where we might be denounced in the Security Council as aggressors, or where the majority of the Assembly were against us.

If Colonel Nasser has done things which are wrong in the legal sense, then, of course, the right step is to take him to the International Court. Indeed, if there were anything which he had done which would justify force at the moment, it is, quite frankly, the one thing on which we have never used force, namely, the stopping of the Israeli ships. We have not done that; and it would, I think, be difficult to find—I must say this—in anything else he has done any legal justification for the use of force. What he may do in the future is another matter.

I come, therefore, to this conclusion. I believe that we were right to react sharply to this move. If nothing at all were done, it would have very serious consequences for all of us, especially for the Western Powers. It is important that what we do should be done in the fullest possible co-operation with the other nations affected. We should try to settle this matter peacefully on the lines of an international commission, as has been hinted. While force cannot be excluded, we must be sure that the circumstances justify it and that it is, if used, consistent with our belief in, and our pledges to, the Charter of the United Nations and not in conflict with them.

18 · Sir Anthony Eden's record of the views of John Foster Dulles at a meeting of the British, French, and American Foreign Secretaries, 1 August 1956

Mr Dulles summed up his views as follows:

1. It was intolerable that the Canal should be under the domination of any single country without any international control;
2. We should use the 1888 Convention as a basis for discussion in order to avoid complications with the Panama Canal;
3. Force was the last method to be tried, but the United States did not exclude the use of force if all other methods failed;
4. We should mobilise world opinion in favour of international operation of the Canal;
5. We should attempt to get our tripartitite views accepted by at least a two-thirds majority of the conference that was to be called.

In further discussion, Mr Dulles said:

A way had to be found to make Nasser disgorge what he was attempting to swallow. . . . We must make a genuine effort to bring word opinion to favour the international operation of the canal. . . . It should be possible to create a world opinion so adverse to Nasser that he would be isolated. Then if a military operation had to be undertaken it would be more apt to succeed and have less grave repercussions than if it had been undertaken precipitately.

19 · Proposals of the First London Conference, 2–23 August 1956

This was the proposal that a committee headed by Sir Robert Menzies took to Egypt and which was refused.

Composition of Board to control the Suez Canal

The members of the board, in addition to Egypt, would be other states chosen in a manner to be agreed upon from among the states parties to the convention with due regard to use, pattern of trade and geographical distribution; the composition of the board to be such as to assure that its responsibilities would be discharged solely with a view to achieving the best possible operating results without political motivation in favour of, or in prejudice against, any user of the canal.[1]

20 · Sir Anthony Eden's telegram to President Eisenhower, late August 1956

This is a message to thank you for all the help Foster has given. Though I could not be at the conference myself, I heard praise on all sides for the outstanding quality of his speeches and his constructive leadership. He will tell you how things have gone. It was, I think, a remarkable achievement to unite eighteen nations on an agreed statement of this clarity and force.

Before he left, Foster spoke to me of the destructive efforts of the Russians at the conference. I have been giving some thought to this and I would like to give you my conclusions.

I have no doubt that the Bear is using Nasser, with or without his knowledge, to further his immediate aims. These are, I think, first to dislodge the West from the Middle East, and second to get a foothold in Africa so as to dominate that continent in turn. In this connection I have seen a reliable report from someone who was present at the lunch which Shepilov gave for the Arab Ambassadors. There the Soviet claim was that they 'only wanted to see Arab unity in Asia and Africa and the abolition of all foreign bases and exploitation. An agreed unified Arab nation must take its rightful place in the world'.

This policy is clearly aimed at Wheelus Field and Habbaniya as well as at our Middle East oil supplies. Meanwhile the communist bloc continue their economic and political blandishments towards the African countries which are already independent. Soon they will have a wider field for subversion as our colonies, particularly in the West, achieve self-government. All this makes me more than ever sure that Nasser must not be allowed to get away with it this time. We have many friends in the Middle East and in Africa and others who are shrewd enough to know where the plans of a Nasser or a Musaddiq would lead them. But they will not be strong enough to stand against the power of the mobs if Nasser wins again. The firmer the front we show together, the greater the chance that Nasser will give way without the need for any resort to force. That is why we were grateful for your policy and Foster's expression of it at the conference. It is also one of the reasons why we have to continue our military preparations in conjunction with our French allies.

We have been examining what other action could be taken if Nasser refuses to negotiate on the basis of the London Conference. There is the question of dues. The Dutch and the Germans have already indicated that they will give support in this respect. The Dutch may even be taking action in the next few days. Then there is the question of currency and economic action. We are studying these with your people and the French in London and will be sending our comments soon. It looks as though we shall have a few days until Nasser gives Menzies his final reply. After that we should

[1]Signed by 18 nations but not by India, Russia, Indonesia, Ceylon.

be in a position to act swiftly. Selwyn Lloyd is telegraphing to Foster about tactics, particularly in relation to the United Nations.

Meanwhile I thought I should set out some of our reflections on the dangerous situation which still confronts us. It is certainly the most hazardous that our country has known since 1940.

21 · Suez Canal Users' Association Sir Anthony Eden's speech in the House of Commons (extract), 12 September 1956

The members of the Users' Association will include the three Governments I have already mentioned—the United States, France and ourselves—and the other principal users of the Canal will be invited to join. We hope that the pattern of membership will be as representative as possible. The Users' Association will employ pilots, will undertake responsibility for the co-ordination of traffic through the Canal, and, in general, will act as a voluntary association for the exercise of the rights of Suez Canal users.

The Egyptian authorities will be requested to co-operate in maintaining the maximum flow of traffic through the Canal. It is contemplated that Egypt shall receive appropriate payment from the association in respect of the facilities provided by her. But the transit dues will be paid to the Users' Association and not to the Egyptian authority. Through this organisation it should be possible to establish a system of transit of the Canal for a substantial volume of shipping. Of course, we recognise that a provisional organisation of this kind, designed to meet an emergency, cannot be in a position to provide for the major developments which are becoming urgently necessary if the Canal is to continue adequately to serve the interests of its users and we also recognise that the attitude of the Egyptian Government will have an important bearing on the capacity of the association to fulfil its functions (Laughter) Yes. But I must make it clear that if the Egyptian Government should seek to interfere—

Mr Harold Davies (Leek): Deliberate provocation

The Prime Minister: —with the operations of the Association, or refuse to extend to it the essential minimum of co-operation, then that Government will once more be in breach of the Convention of 1888. (Hon. Members: 'Resign') I must remind the House that what I am saying—(An Hon. Member: 'What a peacemaker!')—is the result of exchanges of views between three Governments. In that event Her Majesty's Government will be free to take such further steps—

Mr S. O. Davies: What do you mean by that?

The Prime Minister: —as seems to be required.

Mr Davies: You are talking about war.

The Prime Minister: —either through the United Nations, or by other means, for the assertion of their rights.

22 · The Suez Canal Users' Association: John Foster Dulles speaking at a Press Conference, 13 September 1956

Q. Mr Secretary, in the event that we would have to send our vessels around the Cape because the Egyptians refused to co-operate, would we hope that other of the principal ship users would do the same thing rather than resort to force?

A. Well, we have often said, and the President has most authoritatively said, that in his opinion force, if justifiable at all, is only justifiable as a last resort. So, if there are alternatives to the use of force, we believe that they should be fully explored and exhausted.

Q. Mr Secretary, the British Press today says that Britain plans to use an armed convoy to go through the Canal if the Users' Association ships are stopped by Colonel Nasser. Would the United States support Britain in such a venture?
A. Well, I don't know what you mean by 'support'. I have said that the United States did not intend itself to try to shoot its way through the Canal.

23 · Sir Anthony Eden's message to President Eisenhower, 6 September 1956

Thank you for your message and writing thus frankly.

There is no doubt as to where we are agreed and have been agreed from the very beginning, namely that we should do everything we can to get a peaceful settlement. It is in this spirit that we favoured calling the twenty-two power conference and that we have worked in the closest co-operation with you about this business since. There has never been any question of our suddenly or without further provocation resorting to arms, while these processes were at work. In any event as your own wide knowledge would confirm, we could not have done this without extensive preparation lasting several weeks.

This question of precautions has troubled me considerably and still does. I have not forgotten the riots and murders in Cairo in 1952, for I was in charge here at the time when Winston was on the high seas on his way back from the United States.

We are both agreed that we must give the Suez Committee every chance to fulfil their mission. This is our firm resolve. If the committee and subsequent negotiations succeed in getting Nasser's agreement to the London proposals of the eighteen powers, there will be no call for force. But if the committee fails, we must have some immediate alternative which will show that Nasser is not going to get his way. In this connection we are attracted by Foster's suggestion, if I understand it rightly, for the running of the canal by the users in virtue of their rights under the 1888 Convention. We heard about this from our Embassy in Washington yesterday. I think that we could go along with this, provided that the intention was made clear by both of us immediately the Menzies mission finishes its work. But unless we can proceed with this, or something very like it, what should the next step be?

You suggest that this is where we diverge. If that is so I think that the divergence springs from a difference in our assessment of Nasser's plans and intentions. May I set out our view of the position.

In the nineteen-thirties Hitler established his position by a series of carefully planned movements. These began with the occupation of the Rhineland and were followed by successive acts of aggression against Austria, Czechoslovakia, Poland and the West. His actions were tolerated and excused by the majority of the population of Western Europe. It was argued either that Hitler had committed no act of aggression against anyone, or that he was entitled to do what he liked in his own territory, or that it was impossible to prove that he had any ulterior designs, or that the Covenant of the League of Nations did not entitle us to use force and that it would be wiser to wait until he did commit an act of aggression.

In more recent years Russia has attempted similar tactics. The blockade of Berlin was to have been the opening move in a campaign designed at least to deprive the Western powers of their whole position in Germany. On this occasion we fortunately reacted at once with the result that the Russian design was never unfolded. But I am sure that you would agree that it would be wrong to infer from this circumstance that no Russian design existed.

Similarly the seizure of the Suez Canal is, we are convinced, the opening gambit in a planned campaign designed by Nasser to expel all Western influence and interests from Arab countries. He believes that if he can get away with this, and if he can successfully defy eighteen nations, his prestige in Arabia will be so great that he will be able to mount revolutions of young officers in Saudi Arabia, Jordan, Syria and Iraq. (We know that he is already preparing a revolution in Iraq, which is the most stable and progressive.) These new Governments will in effect be Egyptian satellites if not Russian ones. They will have to place their united oil resources under the control of a united Arabia led by Egypt and under Russian influence. When that moment comes Nasser can deny oil to Western Europe and we here shall all be at his mercy.

There are some who doubt whether Saudi Arabia, Iraq, and Kuwait will be prepared even for a time to sacrifice their oil revenues for the sake of Nasser's ambitions. But if we place ourselves in their position I think the dangers are clear. If Nasser says to them. 'I have nationalised the Suez Canal. I have successfully defied eighteen powerful nations including the United States, I have defied the whole of the United Nations in the matter of the Israel blockade. I have expropriated all Western property. Trust me and withhold oil from Western Europe. Within six months or a year, the Continent of Europe will be on its knees before you.' Will the Arabs not be prepared to follow this lead? Can we rely on them to be more sensible than were the Germans? Even if the Arabs eventually fall apart again as they did after the early Caliphs, the damage will have been done meanwhile.

In short we are convinced that if Nasser is allowed to defy the eighteen nations it will be a matter of months before revolution breaks out in the oil-bearing countries and the West is wholly deprived of Middle Eastern oil. In this belief we are fortified by the advice of friendly leaders in the Middle East.

The Iraquis are the most insistent in their warnings; both Nuri and the Crown Prince have spoken to us several times of the consequences of Nasser succeeding in his grab. They would be swept away.

The difference which separates us today appears to be a difference of assessment of Nasser's plans and intentions and of the consequences in the Middle East of military action against him.

You may feel that even if we are right it would be better to wait until Nasser has unmistakably unveiled his intentions. But this was the argument which prevailed in 1936 and which we both rejected in 1948. Admittedly there are risks in the use of force against Egypt now. It is, however clear that military intervention designed to reverse Nasser's revolutions in the whole continent would be a much more costly and difficult undertaking. I am very troubled, as it is, that if we do not reach a conclusion either way about the canal very soon one or other of these eastern lands may be toppled at any moment by Nasser's revolutionary movements.

I agree with you that prolonged military operations as well as the denial of Middle East oil would place an immense strain on the economy of Western Europe. I can assure you that we are conscious of the burdens and perils attending military intervention. But if our assessment is correct, and if the only alternative is to allow Nasser's plans quietly to develop until this country and all Western Europe are held to ransom by Egypt acting at Russia's behest it seems to us that our duty is plain. We have many times led Europe in the fight for freedom. It would be an ignoble end to our long history if we accepted to perish by degrees.

24 · Sir Anthony Eden on Resolution (extract from Eden)

There was always a danger that the passage of time and the multiplication of talk would weaken the resolve of the eighteen powers. The risk of letting Nasser keep his prize might in the end be greater than the risk of using force. The question was, how long we could pursue diplomatic methods and economic sanctions, which very likely would not succeed, before the possibility of military action slipped from our grasp. Winter was approaching, when action would be more difficult and other plans would be called for. On 28 August French forces took up their stations in Cyprus. In a few weeks we should be poised to strike, if we had to strike. It would be very costly to keep up this position indefinitely.

Crisis

1 · The Attack

Chronology

15 October	General Challe visits London to explain the French plan.
	Sir Anthony Eden and Selwyn Lloyd go to Paris.
16 October	Christian Pineau comes to London.
23 October	Israel mobilises.
29 October	Israel attacks across Sinai.
30 October	Anglo–French ultimatum to Egypt and Israel.
31 October	British and French air forces attack Egyptian airfields.
2 November	UN calls for cease-fire: military defeat of the Egyptians.
4 November	Egypt blocks Suez Canal.
5 November	Anglo–French troop parachute into Port Said. Russia threatens use of force against Britain, France and Israel.
6 November	Anglo–French seaborne landing at Port Said. Cease-fire at midnight—with military mission incomplete. France willing but unable to continue the war.
7 November	UN set up United Nations Emergency Force.
22 November	British troops evacuated from Suez.
13 November	UN begin clearing the Canal, an operation which lasts till 25 March 1957.

Sinai and Suez

To Ben-Gurion and the Israeli 'hawks' a defensive war became the logical and necessary way of freeing Israel from her burdens. Such a campaign would have three main purposes: to end, by destroying Gaza bases, fedayun raids on Israel, to free Eilat from blockade by destroying the Egyptian bases overlooking the Tiran Straits, to restore the balance of power in the Middle East in Israel's favour.

Attacking Egypt presented military problems which a war against Syria or Jordan clearly did not. An Israeli force crossing the Sinai Desert would be gravely exposed to Egypt's newly re-equipped air force. Israel's need was to find a powerful ally, able and willing to supply her air force with planes comparable to the Egyptian MIGs.

With England, despite growing hostility to Egypt, Israel's relationship was still uneasy. Memories of the bleak unco-operativeness of the withdrawal on the one hand and of Jewish terrorism on the other still hung over the relationship between the two countries. Furthermore, England wanted above all to maintain her friendly connections in the Arab world; to come openly to Israel's side was to invite losing all her Middle East friends. No such dilemma faced France, desperately at war in Algeria, and angered by Nasser's support to the

Algerians. France's Prime Minister, Guy Mollet, a socialist, could argue that a sister socialist democratic republic was under threat—his clear duty was to help.

Ignoring promises made in the Tripartite Declaration, France, from the summer of 1956 onwards, supplied Israel with arms, with Mystère aircraft in particular, which she needed. France–Israel military planning went ahead. Israel's role was defined to set up a cover for Anglo–French intervention whose purpose was 'to topple Nasser'. Israel was to begin the war by attacking across the Sinai Desert. With their navy the French were to cover the entrance to Israeli ports (the 'ceinture maritime') and for the defence of Israel's cities French fighters were to be based on Lydda airfield.

As late as October Britain's role in this warplot was finally decided. At one point there was the danger that Britain, instead of becoming Israel's secret ally would become her open enemy. To divert attention from her real plans, Israel launched an attack against the Jordanian border village of Kakiliah. Under the terms of the Anglo-Jordanian Treaty, King Hussein immediately applied for assistance to Britain. In response to this appeal, Britain arranged for the despatch of a division from Iraq. The danger was real that Britain would find herself fighting both Israel and Egypt.

Britain's intention to attack Egypt was kept secret from her ambassadors and diplomatic staff abroad. This policy produced its own ironies in the Middle East. As late as 27 October, the British Ambassador to Israel, was solemnly warning Ben-Gurion that if Israel attacked Egypt, he must expect Britain to intervene to fulfil her commitments implied in the Tripartite Declaration.

On the night of 29 October 1956, Israel opened her campaign, Operation Kadesh, against Egypt. The defensive war had begun. The mood of Israeli troops was tinged with mystical elation. Israelis were returning to the heartland of Jewry, to Mount Sinai, the mountain of God, where the Mosaic law was first handed down to the Jews.

The political aims of Israel dominated troop movements (this was never true of the Anglo–French operation where for public relations reasons the landings had to be down the Canal when the real political purpose, the disseating of Nasser, called for an attack on Cairo and Alexandria). The campaign began with the occupation of Egyptian border positions at Ras en-Nakeb, Kuntilla and Kusseima, together with a paratroop drop at the Mitla Pass. At Mitla the paras, sited at the east side were ordered not to move. As General Dayan stressed 'we should try as far as possible to get through the next twenty-four hours without additional battles' for 'the key to our situation is the balance of air strength'. Just how unbalanced that was in the next twenty-four hours his own figures reveal. The Egyptians could muster 200 MIGs and 50 Ilyushin bombers. Against this the Israelis had only 37 Mystères and 42 Meteors and Ouragans.

What Israel awaited was Anglo–French intervention and the aircover this would automatically give. When on 31 October Anglo–French planes bombed Egyptian targets, the Israelis were free to move forward, involving initially a drive towards Bir Rud Selim, in the direction of Ismailia, an objective reached by 2 November.

Of no real military importance in the campaign but politically of supreme importance as the source of the fedayun raiders, the Gaza Strip was invaded and taken on 3 November without much Egyptian resistance. Already from 2 November onwards, the Israelis were concentrating on a much more difficult target, the seat of the blockade, Sharm-el-Sheik, the Egyptian fortified position dominating the Tiran Straits. Israeli forces occupying Kuntilla moved south down the shores of the Gulf of Akaba and from their position at the Parker Memorial (east of Mitla) Israeli paratroops drove towards the Gulf of Suez. At Tor, 105 miles further south, the Israeli army dropped more paratroops for a combined attack on Sharm-el-Sheik.

The drive down the Gulf of Akaba had a carefree, Lawrentian quality about it. It recalled in essence that attack by Lawrence and his Arab irregulars on Akaba in that other desert war. In all, the Israeli force was made up of 200 vehicles and 1,800 men, with sufficient food and water to last them for only five days. Any major mishap in that long 185 miles drive could have brought disaster as no relief could possibly reach them. All down the road, its tarred surface melting in the heat, the triumphant Israelis met Egyptian troops drifting away; nowhere until they reached Sharm-el-Sheik did they meet large-scale resistance. On some parts of the route, the road lay through deep sand. Engines became useless. Manpower alone pushed them on at two and half miles an hour.

On the morning of 4 November with that other verbal battle for a cease-fire raging in the United Nations the Israelis reached Sharm-el-Sheik. It was crucial to capture the position before the UN forced a cease-fire on them. To fail now would rob the whole campaign of much of its purpose. By a combined Air Force/Army operation the gun emplacements one by one were destroyed. At 9.30 on 5 November Sharm-el-Sheik surrendered. Sinai was now in Israel's hands.

The paratroopers' verve carried them further than General Dayan intended: men such as these make their own role and choose their own destiny. Their commanders knew nothing of the bargain struck with England and France. Destination Suez was in their minds. Their orders were clear: they were to stay where they had been dropped at the eastern end of the Mitla Pass. Under cover of sending out a patrol, brigade command despatched a force large enough to capture the Pass. This was the force which ran into largescale fighting, and strafing from Egyptian MIGs. After tough and harassing fighting, the Pass was taken. It was, however, a battle without purpose for Israel had no interest in moving on to the Canal. From Mitla the paratroopers were to be diverted south, towards Sharm-el-Sheik, when Anglo-French aircover made further Israeli moves safe.

France, indeed, went further than providing cover for Israeli forces. During the Suez War, Mystères from the French Air Force were based in Israel, at Lydda and Haifa. From further away, from Cyprus, French carrier planes ferried food, water, petrol, armaments, to the

Israeli paratroops waiting at the Mitla Pass.

The Sinai Campaign, the desert war, with its capture of Sinai, the Tiran Straits, the Gaza Strip, was a major victory for Israel. One of the great prizes Israel brought out of Sinai was the heightened prestige of her army; more unexpectedly and at least as important was the captured Czech and Russian equipment: tanks, self-propelled guns, trucks, petrol. The Egypt–Czech arms deal which initially had altered the balance of power in the Middle East had in effect been undone by the Sinai War.

What perhaps is most striking is the total failure of the Arab states to come to Nasser's assistance. On 23 October, a few days before the Israeli attack, Egypt, Syria and Jordan formed a united military command. Neither Syria or Jordan tried to distract Israel, although it seems Syria was prepared to do so and was restrained by Nasser.

To Israel all was triumph, marred only by innocent Arab deaths at Kafr Kassim, an Israel border village near Jordan. The village was swiftly occupied and a curfew ordered. The headman protested that men working outside the village in the fields would know nothing of the curfew. Over his protests it was imposed and Arabs returning to the village after six o'clock, the hour of curfew, were shot down in the village streets.

The Franco–Israeli conspiracy supported by Great Britain had worked reasonably well. This was the plan revealed to the British Cabinet in early October. The plan was a simple one. Israel was to begin the war. On the cry of 'the Canal in danger' almost identical ultimatums were to be sent to Egypt and Israel calling on them 'to stop all warlike action on land, sea and air forthwith' and then 'to withdraw all forces to a distance of ten miles from the Canal'. This was scheduled for 30 October. By this time Israel would not be anywhere near ten miles from the Canal—the only forces in the area would be Egyptian, operating within their own rightful territory. England and France could then appear not as aggressors but as intermediaries concerned 'to guarantee freedom of transit through the Canal . . . by the temporary occupation of key positions at Port Said, Ismailia and Suez', in a sense almost as minor emissaries of the United Nations.

Israel's quarrel with Egypt had precise and limited military objectives: the Anglo–French quarrel did not. At the El Alamein commemoration in May 1967 (held in Egypt) the victor of El Alamein, Field Marshal Montgomery condemned Suez as 'morally wrong'. The question whether it was also politically and militarily wrong is still being discussed.

From the British side, the quarrel turned partly on personal animosities—Sir Anthony Eden's capacity to see Nasser as another, if smaller, Hitler—and partly on Britain's lingering sense of imperial mission. In the background was British fear of Russian penetration of the Middle East, an area which for fifty years had been almost a British preserve.

For some time American and British diplomacy ran in double harness. The break came at the beginning of October when Dulles realised that the British were prepared to use force outside the framework of the United Nations. The imperative British need to develop a foreign policy independently of her great wartime ally, was intense, almost neurotic. There was, too, a nostalgic attractiveness in the idea of reviving the Entente Cordiale. To France therefore—and away from the United States—the Eden Government turned.

For France the problem was very different. Her North African territories were in revolt and within Algeria, a strong nationalist movement, the FLN was committed to war and terrorism against French control. From Radio Cairo came voluble and violent support for fellow Arabs in Algeria; from Cairo, so the French claimed, came arms for the rebels. Nationalisation of the Canal Company had inflamed French public opinion—Paris after all was still the headquarters of the Universal Canal Company—but the problem, too, for France was that of outmoded imperial attitudes.

In the Middle East, Britain and France had a common purpose: to topple Nasser. Little thought had been given to what would take his place or how long Anglo–French occupation was likely to be. Within the Entente there were differences of attitude which made Franco–Israeli cooperation easier and more open. The French no longer had friends in the Arab world: the British still counted supporters in Jordan and Iraq. There was also the question of oil on which the industry of a modern society depends. With pipelines crossing Syria and oil from the Persian Gulf sheikdoms, Britain's vital oil supplies might be imperilled if Britain openly joined an Israeli attack against Egypt.

The final plans worked out combined three often contradictory objectives: (a) an Israeli attack, basically a large-scale retaliatory raid with specifically Israeli purposes (b) an Anglo–French invasion having as its military purpose the occupation of the Canal and (c) the destruction of the Nasser regime. The missing element in this neat calculation was world opinion, particularly as expressed in the UN. There was an understandable concern to play down what was being done for none of the three wanted an all-out war. Britain and France limited the size of their bombs, the Egyptian population were warned by leaflet and by Radio Cyprus of the intended target areas. This was not seen as major war, merely a salvage operation.

On the evening of 31 October the allied bombardment began. 240 planes attacked Egyptian airfields, an attack which transformed the Sinai expedition's chances for Nasser immediately withdrew forces from Sinai to have them ready against an expected Anglo-French invasion.

Operation Musketeer went on its stately and foreordained way and on 5 November 1956 Anglo–French paratroops landed at Port Said. World opinion had already hardened against the whole campaign. The American Administration had been kept in the dark by Britain and the Anglo–American alliance was under severe strain. There had been no consultations with the Commonwealth. India, in particular, was increasingly critical and Canadian diplomats were anxiously trying to find a way out without too much irreparable loss to Britain and the Commonwealth. Within the United Nations news from the Middle East rivalled the tragic news from Hungary in importance and urgency. An American resolution on 30 October called on Israel 'to withdraw her armed forces behind the established armistice lines' and asked all UN members 'to refrain from giving any military, economic or financial assistance to Israel'. Britain and France vetoed this resolution—and a similar Soviet resolution. On 1 November the General Assembly called for an immediate cease-fire.

Outside the United Nations, Russia took a hand in the diplomatic game by sending a letter to Sir Anthony Eden from Marshall Bulganin. Its tone was bellicose. Bulganin, one of the two leaders of the Russian Government, referred to 'the inhuman attack' against 'a practically defenceless Egypt'. He underlined his willingness to join with other UN powers to use 'naval and air forces in order to end the war in Egypt, and to crush aggression. We are, he said, fully determined to crush the aggressors by the use of force and to restore peace in the East'. There were references to rocket attacks on London and the note ended ominously: 'We hope that at this critical moment you will show due common sense and draw the appropriate conclusions'.

Russia also talked of sending Russian volunteers to the Middle East to defend Egypt. To Israel the greatest diplomatic blow was a Soviet reference to 'a question mark (put) against the very existence of Israel as a state.'

Within the UN Britain and France were isolated and condemned. On 6 November they agreed to a cease-fire. By this time Britain had no friends in Arab lands; the Suez Canal lay blocked by ships sunk by Egypt; the Syrians had blown up oil pipe lines; Macmillan, the Chancellor, had warned his Prime Minister of a disastrous run on sterling. Britain was to take a long time to recover from the Suez affair.

For Arab-Israeli relations, the Suez affair produced the United Nations Emergency Force, commanded by Lt. General Burns from UNTSO, a force which the crisis in confidence produced by Suez was to make possible. UNEF was to mark the beginnings of a peace-keeping force in the Middle East. Sir Anthony Eden was later to claim that this had been one of his objectives. For the Israelis the Suez affair was not a fiasco; the Sinai Campaign, Operation Kadesh, had been uniformly victorious: the homeland of the fedayun had been destroyed and the coastline of the Gulf of Akaba in Israeli hands.

The end of the affair lay with the UN when on 16 March 1957 the Israelis finally moved out of Sinai. The UN had guaranteed that the fedayun raids would end and that Israeli shipping would be free from Egyptian threat in the Tiran Straits. The Secretary-General took responsibility for these guarantees and stationed UNEF forces in the Gaza Strip and at Sharm-el-Sheik. The Israelis refused to allow UN forces on their territory thereby putting themselves at a disadvantage tactically when in May 1967 Nasser successfully secured their removal from Egyptian territory. The UNEF forces moved out leaving control of Akaba once more to Egypt and the Israelis once more back where they were before Suez. It may be argued that the very success of the Israeli invasion told inevitably against Israel in that it inflicted on Egypt—and through her the Arab world—a humiliation similar to that of 1948.

The Sinai Campaign ended the Tripartite Agreement—at least as it concerned Britain and France although as late as May 1967 the Americans were still to claim responsibility in the Middle East on the basis of the Agreement. The actions of Britain and France had brought the Tripartite Agreement into ridicule. In the future Israel—and Egypt—would be free to buy arms in the open market.

25 · General Challe's visit to London
(Anthony Nutting's account),
15 October 1956

I thought for a moment of arguing the obvious point that our obligations stemmed from the Tripartite Declaration itself and that, whatever Egypt might say, this meant that we had a peace-keeping role to play in the Middle East. But it seemed more important to find out what lay behind the French enquiry. So I asked Gazier what, if any, information he had that Israel was contemplating an attack on Egypt. For a moment or two he did not answer, but sat looking nervously at the Private Secretary, who was busily taking notes in the background. Then, when Eden had told his Secretary to stop, Gazier said that he would like General Challe to speak.

Challe then proceeded to outline what he termed a possible plan of action for Britain and France to gain physical control of the Suez Canal. The plan, as he put it to us, was that Israel should be invited to attack Egypt across the Sinai Peninsula and that France and Britain, having given the Israeli forces enough time to seize all or most of Sinai, should then order 'both sides' to withdraw their forces from the Suez Canal, in order to permit an Anglo-French force to intervene and occupy the Canal on the pretext of saving it from damage by fighting. Thus the two powers would be able to claim to be 'separating the combatants' and 'extinguishing a dangerous fire', while actually seizing control of the entire waterway and of its terminal ports, Port Said and Suez. This would not only restore the running of the Canal to Anglo-French management, but, by putting us physically in control of the terminal ports—a position which Egypt had hitherto always held—it would enable us to supervise all shipping movements through the Canal and so to break the Egyptian blockade of Israel.

Nothing was said at this stage about the timing of these operations, although it was made fairly clear to us that the French wanted as little delay as possible. Likewise, the military plan was not discussed in any detail, Challe merely suggesting that a combined sea-borne and paratroop invasion should suffice—the sea-borne operation to take Port Said and the paratroops to seize Ismailia, headquarters of the Suez Canal administration, and Suez. Nor did either Frenchman say definitely that the Israelis had agreed to play their allotted part. But from what Challe told us it was clear that the French had made at least preliminary soundings with the Israeli Government, and that they had been given enough encouragement to follow up with this enquiry as to our likely attitude.

When Challe had finished his brief exposé, Gazier wound up by asking the Prime Minister to let the French Government know as soon as possible what he thought of the French plan.

26 · The Anglo–French meeting in Paris, 16 October 1956

Finally, at our meeting we discussed the situation in the Middle East, its dangers and what we could do. The line-up between Jordan, Egypt and Syria was becoming ever close. There were reports of the establishment of a joint command under Egyptian direction, which in fact soon came into existence. Cairo radio blared with increasing vehemence against Israel, menacing her with destruction. Unless Israel was prepared just to sit and wait until it suited her enemies to strangle and finally destroy her, it was clear that before long she would have to take some counter-action at least to put an end to the fedayeen raids. If directed against Jordan, from which some of the fedayeen raids were said to be mounted under Egyptian leadership, then the position for us would be terrible indeed. We had a treaty obligation to defend Jordan. The Jordanians had no effective air force, our fighter squadrons provided their only protection. Already there had nearly been an incident when, in some counter-raid, an Israeli aircraft had for the first time been engaged. Our help had been called for and our aircraft were on the point of going up, when a wise and rapid exchange of cautionary messages on the spot avoided catastrophe.

Nevertheless, the danger was there. If an attack were launched against Jordan, the Israelis would be using their French Mysteres, the delivery of a number of these having previously been agreed by the United States, France and ourselves, the three partners to the Tripartite Declaration. The Royal Air Force would be in action for Jordan, the United States would be on the sidelines. This was a nightmare which could only too easily come true; Jordan calling for support from Nasser and ourselves, Nasser calling for support from Russia, France lined up with Israel on the other side.

As long ago as January, our Ambassador had warned Jordan that Egyptian interference was highly dangerous for her. Egypt was manoeuvring to embroil Jordan with Israel. If Israel were to act against one of her encircling enemies, the choice lay between Jordan and Egypt. Syria was insufficiently important. Jordan had provided the one effective military force, the Arab Legion, in the fighting of 1948–9. Despite the large supplies of Soviet equipment which the Egyptians had received, the Legion was probably still the most formidable military formation which Israel's neighbours could put into the field. It might be thought imprudent to act against Egypt while leaving the Legion intact. As against this, Egypt was the political source and inspiration of the threat to Israel. It was the Cairo radio which blared out the daily hatred and the incitement to kill. It was Nasser who had thought out the horror of the fedayeen. In the event, Israel found the answer by keeping her best troops in position to cover the front against Jordan, while using less experienced forces for the incursion into Sinai. They proved brilliantly equal to the call upon them.

My colleagues and I were acutely aware of the consequence of action by Israel against Jordan, which we had to do all in our power to avert. Our relations with Israel were not close or intimate, there were constant arguments about the supply of arms. Therefore, at this meeting in Paris, we asked the French Ministers to do everything they could to make clear to Israel that an attack on Jordan would have to be resisted by us. This they undertook to do. It was not only our own treaty engagements which concerned us, but the effect upon Iraq of events in Jordan. To fail to carry out our engagement would be the end of our position in the Middle East, to have to carry it out would be disastrous to Western unity. No dilemma could be more difficult. If Israel were to break out against Egypt and not against Jordan, this dilemma could not arise. For this reason, if there were to be a break out it was better from our point of view that it should be against Egypt. On the other hand, if the break out were against Egypt, then there would be other worries, for example the safety of the Canal. We discussed these matters in all their political and military aspects. In common prudence we had to consider what our action should be, for our two countries were, as we knew, the only powers to have effective military forces at our command in the area. During recent months we had been mounting our military preparations to deal with any interference or other act by Nasser against our ships or our people. Now Nasser's policies were provoking Israel beyond endurance and this also we had to prepare for.

27 · The Paris Meeting:
(Anthony Nutting's account)
16 October 1956

I made one last desperate attempt to buttonhole Lloyd before he set off for Paris. But in vain; Eden insisted on his staying to lunch at No. 10, and I returned alone to nurse my forebodings at the Foreign Office. I managed to reach Lloyd by telephone before he left for the airport, but he was in no mood to listen to my pleadings. Eden had clearly used the lunch interval to devastating effect, for Lloyd not only seemed prepared to acquiesce in the French plan, but now took the line that his agreement with Fawzi would never hold. He conceded that it would be in Egypt's own best interests to work it, as she would gain both the management of the Canal and the lion's share of the dues. But, echoing Eden, he kept repeating that we could not trust Nasser to honour any commitment.

The next day I sought Lloyd out to enquire what had taken place in Paris. He was evasive at first, saying that the talks had been so secret that only the Prime Ministers and Foreign Secretaries had been present and no record had been made. But under cross-examination, he admitted that Eden had confirmed his whole-hearted endorsement of the French plan and that further consultations would take place in Paris between French and Israeli representatives. He hoped that we would not have to be directly associated with these talks, at any rate at the political level; but he could not rule this out, as there were a number of crucial political as well as military problems involving us which would have to be settled in a very short space of time. Lloyd added that the French had clearly been in cahoots with the Israelis for several weeks.

I have seldom seen a man more confused and unhappy than Lloyd was on this occasion. But, since it was clear that he had lost control of the situation and that he was no more able than I to stop Eden plunging ahead, there was nothing to be gained by further argument. All I could do, and this I did, was to tell him very solemnly that, if we went through with this plan, I would have to resign. This would be a bitter experience for me, but I could not stay in the Government if it meant being a party to this sordid conspiracy. And I hoped that he would tell the Prime Minister of what I had said.

Lloyd gave a nervous laugh and, as was his habit when embarrassed, sought refuge in a facetious joke. 'There's only one worse thing than having a yes-man on one's team, and that's having a no-man like you,' he said.

28 · The Sèvres Agreement
(Hugh Thomas's account)

Mollet and Ben-Gurion confirmed at Sèvres on 23 October the Franco–Israeli side of the plan, such as a ceinture maritime of French naval ships along the Israeli coast, an 'umbrella,' of French fighters to protect Israeli cities, and French parachute drops of food, ammunition and trucks to the advancing Israelis by Cyprus-based aircraft. It is not clear to what extent the direct help that France was going to offer to Israel was made known to Britain. That evening the 'responsible British Minister' and an official flew secretly to Paris. A French Minister, in conversation with me, referred to the Minister as the 'British representative'.

Whoever he was, he appeared according to one who was present, like an 'old-fashioned family lawyer'. Seeming to disapprove of the whole project, he keenly argued how it should be most effectively presented. Appearances had to be kept up. The Anglo–French should appear at all times to be defending the Canal against both sides.

Britain had not wanted to begin bombing Egyptian airfields until seventy-two hours after the start of the Israeli offensive; France was ready to start bombing immediately—though of course her bombers would not be mainly responsible. A compromise was reached: thirty-six hours. There would, however, be a British aerial watch over Egyptian airfields from the start. Britain argued that the Israeli attack had to be made to seem not simply a border raid, such as Ben-Gurion had mounted against Jordan. Anything less than a full war could not be said to threaten the Canal and therefore justify the great ruse.

. . . There is no reason to doubt that the British Minister who went to Paris was Lloyd. . .

29 · General Dayan's Diary, 25 October 1956

After numerous internal conferences, and contacts and clarifications with people overseas, which started about two months ago, we can sum up the situation today as follows:

1. The Prime Minister and Minister of Defence, David Ben-Gurion, has given approval in principle to the campaign and its aims.

2. Our forces will go into action at dusk on 29 October 1956, and we must complete the capture of the Sinai Peninsula within seven to ten days.

3. The decision on the campaign and its planning are based on

the assumption that British and French forces are about to take action against Egypt.

4. According to information in our possession, the Anglo–French forces propose to launch their operations on 31 October 1956. Their aim is to secure control of the Suez Canal Zone, and for this they will need to effect a sea landing or an air drop with, no doubt, suitable air cover.

30 · Israel attacks: the official pretext

(Account of Lieut. Gen. Burns)

The Defence Forces' announcement of Israel's attack on Egypt was accompanied by an apologia by the Foreign Ministry spokesman: 'Israel this evening took security measures to eliminate the Egyptian fedayeen bases in the Sinai Peninsula'. The statement went on to allege that within the last week twenty-four Israel casualties, dead and wounded, had been caused by mines placed by the fedayeen in the Southern Negev.

Nearly all the casualties complained of resulted from one incident. Two military vehicles were blown up in the El Auja demilitarised zone, and first reports were that three soldiers had been killed and twenty-seven wounded. Of course, the presence of Israeli soldiers in this zone was in violation of the General Armistice Agreement, and despite repeated demands by the United Nations that Israel withdraw her troops from it. The Israelis, furthermore, had refused to allow UNMOs to investigate this incident, as well as others which the Foreign Ministry statement included under the heading of fedayeen activities in the Negev. As there was no impartial investigation of the facts, it was open to the Israeli authorities, if they wanted a casus belli, to exaggerate or falsify any incident, or even to invent incidents. In this case there is no reason to believe that the incidents the Israelis complained of did not take place. But there is no impartially ascertained evidence that they did, either.

The Foreign Ministry also cited the blocking of the Suez Canal and alleged Egypt had 'gloried in the effort to encompass Israel with a ring of steel with the announced and flaunted purpose at the appropriate moment of annihilating her, crowned a few days ago by a Syrian–Jordan–Egyptian military command under the Egyptian commander-in-chief'.

In short, Israel was initiating the preventive war which Mr Ben-Gurion had declared she never would, with the above justification. Reading this statement, I was reminded again of the words I had heard attributed to Mr Ben-Gurion a year and a half before: that the function of the Ministry of Foreign Affairs was to justify, in the eyes of the world, the actions of the Israeli Defence Force. Perhaps he didn't say it, but in the following eighteen months anyone could have said it, and with justice.

31 · Israel attacks: General Dayan[1] on Anglo–French help

The Anglo–French bombing of Egyptian airfields which started last night has neutralized the capacity of the Egyptian Air Force to operate against us. Even before this, throughout the first night of the campaign (29 October) and the two days of fighting which preceded the Anglo–French action (30 and 31 October) Egyptian

[1]Major-General Dayan was Chief of Staff of the Israeli Army at the time of the Sinai Campaign

air activity did not extend beyond the boundaries of Sinai. The neighbouring Arab states, Syria and Jordan, who were asked to attack Israel from the air and who promised to do so, in fact did nothing. Actually, the Egyptian Air Force did send over Ilyushin-28 bombers on two occasions, on the nights of the 30th and 31st, one bomber on each mission, but they dropped their bombs on open ground, far from city or village, without discrimination and without causing damage.

32 · The public reaction of the British Prime Minister, Sir Anthony Eden, to the news of the Israeli invasion

On 25 October a report came that Israel was about to mobilise. She did so and moved against Egypt on the evening of the 29th. I thought then, and I think now, that the Israelis had justification for their action. It is at least a grim possibility that they would not be a free nation today had they not taken it. The marked victim of the garrotter is not to be condemned if he strikes out before the noose is round his throat.

If we were not prepared to condemn Israel, we could not stand aside and watch events. In an Israel–Egyptian conflict our military advisers expected the Israelis to win; their quality, intelligent training and dedicated courage outmatching the Egyptian advantage in numbers and equipment. The chief peril to us lay not in the conflict but in its extension by the intervention of other Arab states. The best way to halt that was by intervening ourselves. These considerations decided our course of action.

Ministers had already considered at several meetings the ways in which the situation might develop. These had also been canvassed with the French. On 25 October the Cabinet discussed the specific possibility of conflict between Israel and Egypt, and decided in principle how it would react if this occurred. The Governments of France and the United Kingdom should, it considered, at once call on both parties to stop hostilities and withdraw their forces to a distance from either bank of the canal. If one or both failed to comply within a definite period, then British and French forces would intervene as a temporary measure to separate the combatants. To ensure this being effective, they would have to occupy key positions at Port Said, Ismailia and Suez. Our purpose was to safeguard free passage through the canal, if it were threatened with becoming a zone of warfare, and to arrest the spread of fighting in the Middle East.

To realise this we would put into operation the plan for occupation of the Suez Canal zone, prepared by the joint Anglo–French military staff which had been studying the problem since the end of July. An advantage of this course was that we did not need to recast our military preparations. The same plan that had been intended to deal with Nasser's seizure of the canal fitted equally well with our new objective. Critics asked why we landed so far behind the combatant area. The answer is that to land anywhere except as planned would have involved delay and we could not afford delay. We were also limited by shortage of landing craft and had to have the use of a port.

33 · The British ultimatum to Egypt[1], 30 October 1956

The Governments of the United Kingdom and France have taken note of the outbreak of hostilities between Israel and Egypt. This event threatens to disrupt the freedom of navigation through the Suez Canal, on which the economic life of many nations depends. The Governments of the United Kingdom and France are resolved to do all in their power to bring about the early cessation of hostilities and to safeguard the free passage of the Canal. They accordingly request the Government of Egypt:

(a) to stop all warlike action on land, sea and air forthwith;
(b) to withdraw all Egyptian forces to a distance of ten miles from the Canal; and
(c) in order to guarantee freedom of transit through the Canal by the ships of all nations and in order to separate the belligerents, to accept the temporary occupation by Anglo-French forces of key positions at Port Said, Ismailia and Suez.

The United Kingdom and French Governments request an answer to this communication within twelve hours. If at the expiration of that time one or both Governments have not undertaken to comply with the above requirements, United Kingdom and French forces will intervene in whatever strength may be necessary to secure compliance.

34 · Britain's Purpose: Sir Anthony Eden's speech in the House of Commons (extract) 1 November 1956

We best avoid great wars by taking even physical action to stop small ones. Everybody knows that the United Nations is not in a position to do that. We and the French have the forces available. We must face the fact that the United Nations is not yet the international equivalent of our own legal system and the rule of law. . . .

Effective action to re-establish peace will make easier an international solution of the many problems which exist in that area. Of course, we do not delegate to ourselves any special position in that respect. On the contrary we would welcome and look for the participation of many other nations in bringing about a settlement and in upholding it.

Israel and Egypt are locked in conflict in that area. The first and urgent task is to separate these combatants and to stabilise the position. That is our purpose. If the United Nations were then willing to take over the physical task of maintaining peace in that area, no one would be better pleased than we. But police action there must be to separate the belligerents and to prevent a resumption of hostilities.

35 · The attitude of the Opposition: Hugh Gaitskell's speech in the House of Commons, 31 October 1956

. . . In taking this decision the Government, in the view of Her Majesty's Opposition, have committed an act of disastrous folly whose tragic consequences we shall regret for years. (Hon. Members: 'Oh') Yes, all of us will regret it, because it will have done irreparable harm to the prestige and reputation of our country.

Sir, this action involves not only the abandonment but a positive assault upon the three principles which have governed British

[1]A similar ultimatum was sent to Israel.

foreign policy, for, at any rate, the last ten years—solidarity with the Commonwealth, the Anglo–American Alliance and adherence to the Charter of the United Nations. . . .

The Prime Minister said yesterday that he had been in close consultation with the Commonwealth. What were the results of this close consultation? I do not think that there was ever much doubt about what the attitude of the Government of India was likely to be, and we now know. There has now been a special announcement, and in case Hon. Members have not seen it, I will read it, stating that the Government of India considers Israel's aggression and the ultimatum of Britain and France a flagrant violation of the United Nations Charter and opposed to all the principles of the Bandung Conference.

I do not think that there is much doubt that substantially the same attitude is likely to be adopted by Pakistan and Ceylon. But it is not only the Asian members of the Commonwealth who are concerned. There are the older Dominions. It is remarkable and most distressing fact that Australia was unable to support us in the United Nations Security Council. On one resolution Australia abstained, on the other resolutions she voted against us. The Australian government have said that they are still not in sufficient command of the facts to be able to make a full statement. So it does not seem as though the close consultation has been so very close after all.

The Canadian Government, through the mouth of their Foreign Secretary, have expressed in the coldest possible language their regret at the situation which has arisen. They have also made it plain, through Mr Pearson, that they were not consulted in advance before this ultimatum was sent. The New Zealand Prime Minister has said, in substantially the same words as the Canadian Foreign Minister, that he regrets the situation which has arisen, and that he was unable to say whether he supported the United Kingdom or not.

This is a tragic situation. . . .

We, as Her Majesty's Opposition, have had to consider what attitude we should adopt to the war on which the Government have so recklessly embarked; we understand, let me say, the gravity of the decision we have to take.

I must now tell the Government and the country that we cannot support the action they have taken and that we shall feel bound by every constitutional means at our disposal to oppose it. . . .

Three eye-witness accounts:

36 · An Englishman in Cairo

On a Tuesday night, a young Egyptian reporter, discussing the news that had just come through of the Israeli attack in the Sinai Desert, remarked: 'Britain, France, and America must now surely stop this aggression against us. Perhaps it will even help bring about a solution of the Suez Canal dispute'.

At that moment an Englishman on the far side of the room gave a shout. We went over to where he was standing watching the Reuter ticket. Sir Anthony Eden's ultimatum was coming up. People couldn't believe what they read; they said nothing, at first. But few Egyptians were slow in believing that the ultimatum to Egypt and Israel was exploiting the Israeli attack for the bases motive: occupation of the Canal Zone—collusion was mentioned straightaway. We went out into the soft night and back to our hotels and houses, feeling that anything was possible.

'What answer could Nasser have given to the British and French ultimatum, except "We resist" '? was the reaction of young Egyptians next day.

Air-raid warnings in Cairo and bursts of anti-aircraft fire over the city caused no great stir. Sudanese servants bellowed 'Noor' (lights) when the sirens sounded. Soon they were shouting 'Noor' in blacked-out hotel corridors in the heat of the day; it didn't seem quite right for Englishmen, even if interrupted in their reading to protest at this.

In the middle of one of the first night raids, someone said he had just heard over Cyprus Radio that Mr Selwyn Lloyd, the Foreign Secretary, had told the House of Commons it was 'untrue that Cairo had been bombed'. Since Cairo is very concentrated, and military targets in the suburbs were not far from the centre of the city, Mr Lloyd's denial sounded a little academic.

In the bar of the hotel, lit by a dim blue light, the correspondent of *The Times* softly played his guitar and sang the sad words of *The Foggy Foggy Dew.*

One relation at this time was to see how they were getting on with the burning of secret papers up at the British Embassy. The Embassy staff had been cut to a minimum, and red-faced figures in PT shorts and gym shoes were burning giant mounds of papers. 'The funeral pyre of British integrity,' remarked a spectator.

The British Ambassador, Sir Humphrey Trevelyan, was making his last official calls in an open khaki Buick with the usual Egyptian police guard. The sound of the bombs had been his first intimation of our attack. Normally he rode around in a black-and-yellow Rolls-Royce like a wasp. 'Thank God he's not using the Rolls today,' someone remarked 'Its colour just about sums up British intentions in the eyes of Egyptians now.'

One afternoon the air-raid hooters sounded and guns opened up: there was a sound of jet aircraft flying low, followed by a mighty crump: two fighter-bombers, flying at about eight hundred feet, appeared in a climbing turn, followed by black puffs of anti-aircraft fire. Against the sun, they appeared to be twin-boomed. Shrapnel rained on the flat dusty roofs of small shops below; word went round that the heaviest explosion was a plane crashing half a mile away. Was it an English pilot?

A young Egyptian, roused from his afternoon sleep, appeared in pyjamas on the balcony of the seedy tenement opposite. He smiled and shrugged.

'What are you doing to us?' asked a small Egyptian downstairs in the foyer of the hotel. He was a university professor and had a Scots wife. He had been in London during the blitz. A jet sliced overhead and his small daughter slid down into her chair and put her fingers in her ears. It wasn't easy to answer the small man's question.

At dusk, a Sudanese in white robe and skull-cap came up with me on to the hotel roof high above Cairo. He was a simple man. We looked out over the city in the soft light, over the strange complex of sand-coloured buildings, to the slender minarets of the mosque of Mohammed Ali, and beyond to the bare grey Moqattam Hills. Pillars of smoke from burning airfields and fuel dumps stained the sky.

The Sudanese spoke a slow Arabic. 'Are you English?' he asked. 'Only four countries are with England. I read it in the paper.'

The next morning, the fourth day of bombing, a large party of foreign correspondents toured bombed areas. We drove deep into the country, through groves of tall palm trees that looked almost prehistoric. There were fields of sweet corn, mud huts, peasant women in black robes, small, padding children, astonished buffalo.

Guns opened up, we pulled into the side of the road. English Venoms, well ahead of anti-aircraft bursts, were dive-bombing. It was an odd feeling.

We visited the wireless masts at Abu Zaabal. Two were down. We were beginning to feel that casualties must be small. But there had been six direct hits on the criminal prison next door: stone buildings were flattened, and bodies lay in the hot sun beside craters filled with scummy water.

Once the Egyptian Information Department took us out under armed guard and showed us a film of the effects of the British attack on Port Said. There were shots of the bodies of dead women and children. Afterwards the lights went on, and we sat blinking and feeling none too good. Only our senior colleague felt like speaking: he produced his eye-glass and demanded of an Egyptian official: 'Now look here, when's that doctor coming to see about my dysentery?'

I shall not forget the humanity of the Egyptians throughout the Suez affair. A young typist, mother of twins, remarked during the bombing: 'Oh, I'm worried all right. But it's only crackpots in the office who say things against individual Englishmen'.

At last, after one false alarm, we were told that we were to be expelled.

In the aircraft from Cairo to Naples, we dozed, lulled by the engines. Most of us were to some extent refugees. At Naples we changed planes for Zurich. As we climbed steeply to avoid bad weather over the Alps, the Swiss stewardess, digging in her heels against the slope, came down the cabin, distributing English newspapers: the first we had seen for a month. An account of a debate in the House of Commons caught the eye, with the faces of 'Suez Group' Conservatives smiling confidently from the page. They were discussing clearance of the Canal and withdrawal of British troops. It wasn't easy to concentrate, but one paragraph stuck in the mind:

'Mr Butler (answering a question): "No, sir, I think the honour of our country is safely in the keeping of the Government".'

37 · An Israeli soldier

a) The nature of the Israeli paratroopers

The paratroopers are young and tough, commandos trained to a fine edge. All in this particular Brigade of Israel's Airborne Forces, are volunteers. Their strength lies not in numbers but in fighting fitness, and in this sense they are an élite of the nation, a small race apart within Israel's new race of soldiers. If the airmen are a noble order, hardy and distinguished by a kind of RAF blandness, the paratroopers are a more robust fraternity, picked for physical stamina and intelligence, not by education, and in a way comparable for endurance and toughness, to American Marines. A good many of them come from the land....

The paratroopers have their particular slang and scale of values, in which everyone, by his deeds, is judged 'a man'—but that is the commonest, since they are all 'men' who are not weeded out of the Brigade—or at the other end of the scale, a 'panther', a 'tiger' or a 'lion'. Yehuda is a lion, no question of that. So are many of his Battalion Commanders and aides—the broadshouldered Abraham with his brown eyes and pleasant looks; blue-eyed Nimrod, a striking figure with his reddish beard, very tall and lean, with a hunched bear-like gait, and a lazy, languorous expression: Joseph, stoutish, with fair hair beneath his helmet. The slender Gideon with his razor sharp features and his two lines engraved about the mouth, is, in the opinion of his men, deserving of the highest accolade, 'a considerable male', denoting admiration for his virility in battle.

There are many of them now, these dark and fair boys, selfless and adventurous, who want to be in on the forcing of the Mitla Pass. So, the fortunes of battle still smiling on their unlined young faces, it is in a spirit of elation that they will go on this ride. To them, it is the final move towards Suez, and they want to be the first Israelis, as they might be, to appear on the Canal. Tired they are, but with verve they take their guns, ready half-tracks and mortars, haul ammunition.... A commotion of joking, shouting male ebullience.

b) The performance of the Egyptian army in the action at Mitla Pass

Of the valour of the paratroopers, a hint has already been given. Of the Egyptians in the Mitla Pass it must be said that they fought with courage; not cleverly or with imagination, but rather with the fierceness of despair. They were some five to six hundred men in favoured, dominating positions over the precipice, enjoying the advantage of surprise. In the beginning, too, the Israelis were outnumbered—the column that drove into the wadi was a little under two hundred strong—and they were a long time in the evil canyon before they could be reinforced to anywhere near a size matching the enemy's. Surprise the enemy exploited, shooting hell-for-leather from superior ensconcements, but making no attempt at inspired or imaginative use of his advantage. The Egyptian soldier, under certain not too modern conditions, is a good fighter—good at sabotage, guerilla and similar kinds of warfare based upon hunting instincts, patience, inventivness and skill; he is easily demoralised by mechanical and mass warfare, with its psychological scares. When demoralised he panics and takes to his heels, officers first: there is no good NCO class to give him backbone. But when the going is good he is courageous enough to lie on his back and shoot at 'planes with a rifle.

The result is an uneven army, and explains the variable and often weak Egyptian stand on most other fronts in Sinai.

c) The battle at Mitla Pass, 31 October 1956

Of the terror striking from above.

The hot afternoon dragged on, gruelling and interminable in the narrow gorge. The sun changed its position several times. Iridescent light as well as mauve and dark shadows began to play on the ledges and little pink balconies rising in stories to the high points of the cliffs. At a quarter to four, out of the single clean wedge of blue above, four Egyptian Meteor jets appeared over the rockland, and six MIGs.

At Group Two, Abraham and his officers ordered the men sitting ready in the half-tracks to jump. The drivers took the half-tracks to the side of the road hugging the foothills. The wounded were carried to a cave in the rock, the men took cover in the folds of the hill-side. Four Meteors and two of the MIGs came nosing down over the gully, the other MIGs hovered up high. One good soldier, the one called Moshe, saw a Meteor diving; his luck holding fast, a napalm bomb fell a dozen yards from him without exploding. But on the whole the jets left Group Two pretty well alone, attacking further back along the vicious stretch of all these happenings.

Ury, the reporter, saw the four Meteors all of a sudden from where he crouched with Joseph's little force at the bottom of the wadi. They shrieked down low and so fast that none about Ury could see the markings, and such was their surprise, and their hope that the planes might be 'ours', that they stood up, exposed and gaping. It is just possible it was this that saved them as the pilots may have though they were Egyptians, or, more likely, the pilots knew that 'theirs' and the Israelis were inextricably mixed down under. They rose a wee bit and sought their target, probably with ground-direction, several hundred yards further east, just behind the bend where there were no Egyptians, and only Gideon's companies by the mortars on the incline held by Group Three.

Ury saw the 'planes diving over that close but invisible hill, and with a sinking feeling heard terrible explosions, but first he saw the smoke bursting high over the ridge. Then he saw the two MIGs going in to dive too, and his stomach turned. A shiver went through his body, and he bit his lips, his heart contracting for his paratrooper friends milling about that wretched open hill.

There, a couple of ammunition trucks standing on the road had exploded with an impact shaking the wadi. Somewhere high in the sky a pair of Israeli Mysteres engaged the superior MIGs over the canyon, and but for this harassing a worse and terrible holocaust might have ensued; but even so the Meteors were free to go in unmolested. Three times they dived over Group Three, which so far had been out of danger, hurling bombs, rockets and destruction, mainly on the vehicles. The ambulance with three ill-fated occupants was perforated like a sieve. The troops hung on to the steep cliff-side, and seven were killed, many more wounded. The whole visitation lasted ten minutes.

38 · A National Serviceman: the face of intervention, 29 December 1956

Of course, lots of people have invaded Egypt, but I doubt if many army commanders (except perhaps Antony) have had to board their home-going ships and announce straight away: 'Some of you may wonder what all this has achieved.' That General Stockwell did that shows that the military mind—if less agile than the politician's—is also perhaps more honest.

But, in fact, it was probably difficult for him to do otherwise. For the army officer all along was the one man who had no doubts. Ever since last spring, colonels at selection boards, majors at T.A. drill halls, retired captains at Old Comrades' Association dinners, have been quite certain that the first international priority was to 'give that pip-squeak Nasser a damn good kick in the pants.' And as just eight weeks ago we sailed out for Suez no one on the officers' verandah deck doubted for one moment that that was what the whole business was about.

Hence, every morning the 'battle-warmers' for the troops, the constantly reiterated references to 'a little tea-party with the wogs', and the countenances contorted with fury as Mr Gaitskell's voice ('just like Haw-Haw') came crackling over the wireless set one hot Sunday Mediterranean night. Hence also, six weeks later, the complete and almost comic loss of control on the part of a veteran company commander when, back in our own home barrack town, a small child observed: 'What, were you kicked out or something?'

Throughout, in fact, from the moment when on Sunday, 11 November, the armada's conquering progress was interrupted by an enforced and solemn silence in memory of the dead of two world wars, the whole adventure had an air of unreality. It probably reached its apothesis at El Cap—though I remember thinking at the time that the sight of British majors striding the streets of Port Said and arresting men because they thought that they had suspicious faces was fantastic enough.

At El Cap, however, one stepped straight through the looking glass. There were the trenches, the tumblersful of whisky, the guttering hurricane lamps, even the occasional fall-in of a roof—all the props, in fact, for a repertory run of *Journey's End*. But no theatrical performance could ever have been quite so phoney as this military exercise. In slit trenches impossibly sited in echelon were, for a week at a time, some 900 men—each personally briefed, depite the planned advance, that there was one thing that he must never in any circumstances do: and that was fire a shot. 600 yards away were the Egyptians, with presumably the same orders but with less discipline in carrying them out. And, to hold the ring, there were the white ambulance-looking cars gliding between the lines. They were impressively marked 'UN,' and at their coming road blocks melted away and sentries stood aside.

Also, of course, there were the reporters, almost an army by themselves. Expansive men in expensive service-dress hats, they roared up the Canal and Treaty roads, in fast, comfortable cars, aggressively brandishing their cards, as if the whole thing was a desert carnival laid on for their exclusive benefit. Only the sight of four intruding foreign journalists, morosely marooned and guarded in their car on the roadside, was a reminder that armed conflict, too, could claim its victims. But even they had by the end succeeded in persuading their guards that the whole thing was a joke, of which they were the perpetrators and we the victims.

More seriously, of course, back in Port Said the intervention did claim its casualties. It is all very well to write warm, human, reassuring news stories about the incidentals—the tiny child with the Naafi sweet, the irrepressible mongrel-men with the postcards of international appeal, the triumphant resistance offered (according to the *Daily Sketch*) by British troops in face of temptations laid in their paths by 'the purveyors of sin'. But the coin did have another side; and, as one saw wordly goods being wheeled about in little barrows, the Thersites-like scavengers among the rubble, and Egyptian women fighting and scratching for food, it was impossible not to remember Sir Anthony Eden in August: 'Our quarrel is not with the Egyptian people.'

It was, anyway, clear from the start that their quarrel was now with us; and with one-third of the Arab town destroyed, all the admirable modern hospitals and schools taken over for barracks, and every complaint or protest waved away with a lordy reference to a virtually non-existent Ministry of Civil Affairs, it could scarcely have been otherwise. Later on, of course, things got better; and when, after ten days at El Cap, we returned to Port Said it seemed—with the smiles for the bright blue helmets and the shutters opening remorselessly everywhere to reveal huge and handsome photographs of Nasser—as if a city had awoken from the dead. But it still seems disturbingly appropriate that the last words I heard on Egyptian soil were: 'If I find any of you men talking to these wog children, I'll put you straight inside.' They came from a British company commander; and in a way, perhaps, they provided the answer to General Stockwell's question. For the last glimpse I had of the Gateway to the East—a city where people used professionally to smile—was of fists being shaken from the quay-side as the sun shone on a wreck-studded harbour.

39 · Casualties

On the morning of 7 November the Anglo-French forces were firmly in command of Port Said and fighting had stopped, except for isolated clashes. We had cleared the causeway and advanced as far as El Cap. The total number of men landed in our operation was 22,000, of whom 13,500 were British. Our casualties were sixteen killed and ninety-six wounded and the French ten killed and thirty-three wounded.

The Egyptians circulated wildly exaggerated stories about their casualties. The President of the Law Society, Sir Edwin Herbert, later carried out a thorough investigation into the facts at the request of the Minister of Defence. His findings upon the mission to Port Said, published on 22 December, were that the Egyptians has lost six hundred and fifty dead and had had nine hundred wounded and detained in hospital.

. . . Israeli losses were one hundred and eighty killed and four captured. The Egyptians lost one thousand men killed in action and six thousand prisoners.

2 · World Opinion

The Soviet Attitude

40 · The Soviet reply to an invitation to the First London Conference, 9 August 1956

According to the three-power statement, the composition of the conference has been governed by two principles: parties to the convention of 1888 and nations 'largely concerned in the use of the Canal'. Neither of these principles has been observed, however. Austria–Hungary and Germany were among the signatories to the convention of 1888. Austria, Hungary, Czechoslovakia and Yugoslavia are the successor states of Austria–Hungary. None of these nations has been invited to the conference. Only one part of Germany—the Federal Republic of Germany—has been invited, while the other part—the German Democratic Republic—has not. One cannot agree to this, the more so since the aforementioned states are no less interested in the freedom of navigation through the Suez Canal than the others.

Nor have the Arab nations—Syria, the Lebanon, Saudi Arabia, Jordan, the Sudan, Libya, the Yemen, Iraq, Morocco, Tunisia whose territories are directly adjacent to the Canal and who are vitally interested in having the matter properly settled—been invited to the conference. It should be pointed out that the majority of the Arab nations are likewise the successor states of the former Ottoman Empire, a signatory to the convention of 1888.

Nor have such maritime nations as the Chinese People's Republic, Poland, Bulgaria, Rumania, Burma and Finland, which make extensive use of the Canal, been invited to the conference.

Thus, the conference scheduled to meet in London will be a conference of a group of nations holding shares in the Suez Canal Company, with another group of nations which these principal shareholders of the company have arbitrarily selected.

The Soviet government considers that the aforementioned conference, due to its composition and also to its character and purposes, cannot in any way be regarded as an international meeting authorised to take any decisions whatsoever affecting the Suez Canal.

The Soviet Government considers as most appropriate that the problems connected with ensuring the freedom of navigation through sea canals and straits of international significance should be discussed within the framework of the United Nations.

41 · Mr Shepilov's statement at the First London Conference dissenting from the 18 Power proposals (extract) 21 August 1956

On the eve of the conference, and even in its initial stage, some persons alleged that the nationalisation of the Suez Canal Company by Egypt was an illegal act, that this act in fact violated the provisions of international law, and so forth. This approach is now no longer in evidence. In substance, nobody now disputes the legality of the nationalisation of the Suez Canal Company by the Egyptian government.

Quite recently it was alleged that Egypt's nationalisation of the Suez Canal Company annulled the 1888 Convention and placed the free navigation of the Canal in doubt. The facts show that in spite of the disruptive activities of the former private Suez Canal Company, the operation of the Canal is normal, the volume of traffic and the number of ships passing through the Canal not only has not diminished since nationalisation, but has even increased in comparison with the corresponding period of last year. The Egyptian government has reaffirmed its complete determination to implement the principles of the 1888 Convention, honouring the obligations assumed.

One cannot fail to take into account the fact that an attempt to turn over the operation of the Suez Canal to an international body would mean discriminating against Egypt and, consequently, throwing down a challenge to the Egyptian people who are vigilantly safeguarding their newly acquired national rights. According to a *France Presse* report, the Egyptian government stated on 18 August that they will never agree to the setting up of an international body to operate the Suez Canal and that the setting up of such a body would violate the sovereignty of Egypt and offend her dignity.

The very setting up, contrary to Egypt's desires, of an international body to administer Egyptian property, would constitute a political act which would have serious political consequences. That act would not in any way settle the Suez problem, but it would undoubtedly, turn the Suez Canal area into a zone of constant tension and into a source of international friction and conflict.

Freedom of navigation for all ships of any nation must be securely guaranteed by a new international agreement based on the principles of the 1888 Convention and conforming to the new circumstances and the spirit of the times.

This international agreement might contain, for instance, the following principle provisions:

1. The Suez Canal shall for all time be free and open for the passage of merchant and naval vessels of all states on the basis of equality as regards navigation and port charges and all conditions of navigation. The Canal shall not be used for political purposes to the advantage or detriment of any state interested in navigation through the Canal.

2. Egypt, under whose sovereignty and in whose ownership and operation the Canal is, shall undertake:

(a) To take all necessary measures to ensure complete freedom of navigation through the Suez Canal and to protect the Canal and its installations against any violations of freedom of navigation;

(b) To maintain the Canal in a proper navigable condition which will meet the requirements of navigation and will be in keeping with modern technical standards;

(c) To carry out works to improve the navigation conditions required to increase the passage capacity of the Suez Canal, so that the volume of traffic may be increased in the interests of world trade and of Egypt;

(d) To submit appropriate information to the United Nations on the operation of the Suez Canal.

3. All parties to the Agreement shall undertake not to resort under any circumstances to action which might infringe the inviolability of the Suez Canal or inflict material damage on the installations, offices buildings and works on the Canal.

In conformity with the provisions of the 1888 Convention, the Suez Canal shall never be a theatre of hostilities; no hostile act, nor any act having as its object the obstruction of free navigation of the Canal and its ports of access, shall be permitted; the Canal shall not be subjected to a blockade.

42 · Soviet statement on the aggression against Egypt, 31 October 1956

Egypt has fallen victim to aggression. Her territory has been invaded by Israeli forces and she faces the danger of a landing by British and French forces.

The Israeli forces crossed the Egyptian frontier on the night of 29 October and opened an offensive along the Sinai Peninsula in the direction of the Suez Canal.

The action of the Israeli government constitues armed aggression and an open breach of the United Nations Charter. The facts indicate that the invasion by the Israeli forces has clearly been calculated to be used as an excuse for the Western powers, primarily Britain and France, to bring their troops into the territory of the Arab states, notably, into the Suez Canal zone. To cover up their aggressive actions, the Western powers are invoking the colonialist declaration of 1950 by the United States of America, the United Kingdom and France, which has been unanimously rejected by all the Arab states. The government of Israel, operating as a tool of imperialist circles bent on restoring the regime of colonial oppression in the East, has challenged all the Arab peoples, all the peoples of the East fighting against colonialism. The course which the extremist ruling circles of Israel have taken is a criminal one and dangerous, above all to the state of Israel itself and to its future.

Following the armed attack by Israel, the governments of the United Kingdom and France presented an ultimatum to Egypt on 30 October, demanding key positions for their forces on Egyptian territory—in Suez, Port Said and Ismailia—for the alleged purpose of preventing hostilities between Israel and Egypt. In spite of the fact that the government of Egypt, acting in defence of the country's sovereignty and territorial integrity, has rejected this demand, Britain and France have dispatched their troops for landing on Egyptian territory. The governments of the United Kingdom and France have thus taken the course of armed intervention against Egypt, riding roughshod over the legitimate rights of the sovereign Egyptian state.

This line of action by the governments of the United Kingdom and France is incompatible with the principles and purposes of the United Nations, is a gross violation of the solemn commitments of the member-states of the United Nations, and constitutes an act of aggression against the Egyptian state.

The government of the Soviet Union resolutely condemns the act of aggression against Egypt by the governments of Britain, France and Israel. The freedom-loving peoples of the world fervently sympathise with the Egyptian people waging a just struggle in defence of their national independence.

The Soviet Government considers that the Security Council of the United Nations must, for the sake of preserving peace and tranquillity in the Near and Middle East, take prompt measures towards ending the aggressive actions of Britain, France and Israel against Egypt, and towards the immediate withdrawal of the interventionist forces from Egyptian territory.

The Soviet government holds that all responsibility for the dangerous consequences of these aggressive actions against Egypt will rest entirely with the governments which have taken the line of disturbing peace and security, the line of aggression.

43 · Extract from Mr Shepilov's note to the President of the Security Council, 5 November 1956

The government of the Union of Soviet Socialist Republics proposes the following draft resolution of the Security Council;

'The Security Council

'Bearing in mind that the resolution adopted by the special emergency session of the General Assembly of 2 November 1956, and recommending the governments of the United Kingdom, France and Israel immediately to put an end to the military operations against Egypt and to withdraw their forces from Egyptian territory, has not been implemented by the aforementioned states and that the military operations against Egypt continue,

'Proceeding from the need of taking immediate measures to curb the aggression against Egypt unleashed by the United Kingdom, France and Israel,

'Proposes to the governments of the United Kingdom, France, and Israel that they immediately, but not later than twelve hours after the adoption of this resolution, discontinue all military operations against Egypt and within three days withdraw the troops that have invaded Egyptian territory.

'The Security Council, in conformity with Article 42 of the United Nations Charter, considers it necessary that all the United Nations member-states, and primarily the United States and the USSR, as permanent members of the Security Council which have powerful air and naval forces, render armed and other assistance to the victim of aggression, the Egyptian Republic, by dispatching naval and air forces, military units, volunteers, instructors and *matériel* and other aid if the United Kingdom, France and Israel do not comply with this resolution in the stated time'[1]

The Soviet government, on its part, declares its readiness to make its contribution to curbing the aggressors, to defending the victims of aggression and restoring peace, by dispatching to Egypt the necessary air and naval forces.

[1]The Soviet draft resolution was rejected by the Security Council

44 · Extract from a letter sent by Mr Bulganin to Sir Anthony Eden, 5 November 1956

There is no justification for the fact that the armed forces of Britain and France, two great powers that are permanent members of the Security Council, have attacked a country which only recently acquired its national independence and which does not possess adequate means for self-defence.

In what situation would Britain find herself if she were attacked by stronger states, possessing all types of modern destructive weapons? And such countries could, at the present time, refrain from sending naval or air forces to the shores of Britain and use other means—for instance, rocket weapons. Were rocket weapons used against Britain and France, you would, most probably, call this a barbarous action. But how does the inhuman attack launched by the armed forces of Britain and France against a practically defenceless Egypt differ from this?

With deep anxiety over the developments in the Near and Middle East, and guided by the interests of the maintenance of universal peace, we think that the government of Britain should listen to the voice of reason and put an end to the war in Egypt. We call upon you, upon Parliament, upon the Labour Party, the trade unions, upon the whole of the British people: Put an end to the armed aggression; stop the bloodshed. The war in Egypt can spread to other countries and turn into a third world war.

The Soviet government has already addressed the United Nations and the President of the United States of America with the proposal to resort, jointly with other United Nations member-states, to the use of naval and air forces in order to end the war in Egypt and to curb aggression. We are fully determined to crush the aggressors by the use of force and to restore peace in the East.

We hope that at this critical moment you will show due common sense and draw the appropriate conclusions.

45 · Extract from a letter sent by Mr Bulganin to Sir Anthony Eden, 15 November 1956

You remember, of course, that during our meetings in London and in our personal correspondence we drew your attention in the most friendly way to the dangerous consequences for the United Kingdom in the event of aggressive military actions being started against Egypt. We regret that you did not pay any attention to this at the time. But what has been the result of the intervention against Egypt? Many calamities have been brought upon Egypt—Egyptian towns and villages have been destroyed, thousands of innocent people have been killed or maimed, serious damage has been done to the Suez Canal, and Egypt's trade and economy have been impaired.

But Britain has not achieved anything either by the war against Egypt; she has only suffered heavy damage both politically and economically. The war has closed the Suez Canal to the ships of Britain and other countries, has deprived Britain of a great part of the Middle East oil, has confronted her with large military expenditures and internal economic difficulties. The war has undermined international positions of Britain, aroused the profound hatred of Arab and other peoples of Asian and African countries against the states that took the path of aggression, and worsened Britain's relations with many countries. There can hardly be any doubt that all this will have an unfavourable effect in Britain for a long time.

Justice demands that Britain, France and Israel recompense Egypt for all the damage done as a result of the destruction of Egyptian towns and inhabited localities, the stopping of the functioning of the Suez Canal and the demolition of its structures. The Soviet Government considers it necessary that a special commission be set up with the participation of Egypt to consider and satisfy as soon as possible, Egypt's lawful claims for compensation for the damage done by the military operations of Britain, France and Israel.

The US Attitude

46 · Statement by President Eisenhower on the Middle East including the Israeli Mobilisation, 28 October 1956

During the last several days I have received disturbing reports from the Middle East. These included information that Israel was making a heavy mobilisation of its armed forces. These reports became so well authenticated that yesterday morning, after a meeting with the Secretary of State I sent a personal message to the Prime Minister of Israel expressing my grave concern and renewing a previous recommendation that no forcible initiative be taken which would endanger the peace.

I have just received additional reports which indicate that the Israeli mobilisation has continued and has become almost complete with consequent stoppage of many civil activities. The gravity of the situation is such that I am dispatching a further urgent message to Prime Minister Ben-Gurion.

I have given instructions that these developments be discussed with the United Kingdom and France which joined with the United States in the Tripartite Declaration of 25 May 1950 with respect to the maintenance of peace in the Middle East.

While we have not heard of such large scale mobilisation in countries neighbouring Israel which would warrant such Israeli mobilisation, I have also directed that my concern over the present situation be communicated to other Middle East states urgently requesting that they refrain from any action which could lead to hostilities.

The Security Council of the United Nations now has before it various aspects of the maintenance of peace in the Middle East.

I earnestly hope that none of the nations involved will take any action that will hinder the Council in its efforts to achieve a peaceful solution.

47 · Extract from a Radio and Television Report by President Eisenhower to the American People on the Developments in Eastern Europe and the Middle East, 31 October 1956

I now turn to that other part of the world where, at this moment, the situation is sombre. It is not a situation that calls for extravagant fear or hysteria. But it invites our most serious concern.

I speak, of course, of the Middle East. This ancient crossroads of the world was, as we all know, an area long subject to colonial rule. This rule ended after World War II, when all countries there won full independence. Out of the Palestinian mandated territory was born the new State of Israel.

These historic changes could not, however, instantly banish animosities born of the ages. Israel and her Arab neighbours soon found themselves at war with one another. And the Arab nations showed continuing anger towards their former colonial rulers, notably France and Great Britain.

The United States—through all the years since the close of World War II—has laboured tirelessly to bring peace and stability to this area.

We have considered it a basic matter of United States policy to support the new State of Israel and at the same time—to strengthen our bonds both with Israel and with the Arab countries. But, unfortunately through all these years, passion in the area threatened to prevail over peaceful purposes, and in one form or another, there has been almost continuous fighting.

This situation recently was aggravated by Egyptian policy including rearmament with Communist weapons. We felt this to be a misguided policy on the part of the Government of Egypt. The state of Israel, at the same time, felt increasing anxiety for its safety. And Great Britain and France feared more and more that Egyptian policies threatened their 'life line' of the Suez Canal.

These matters came to a crisis on 26 July of this year, when the Egyptian Government seized the Universal Suez Company. For ninety years—ever since the inauguration of the Canal—that Company has operated the Canal, largely under British and French technical supervision.

Now there were some among our allies who urged an immediate reaction to this event by the use of force. We insistently urged otherwise, and our wish prevailed—through a long succession of conferences and negotiations for weeks—even months—with participation by the United Nations. And there, in the United Nations, only a short while ago, on the basis of agreed principles, it seemed that an acceptable accord was within our reach.

But the direct relations of Egypt with both Israel and France kept worsening to a point at which first Israel—then France—and Great Britain also determined that, in their judgement, there could be no protection of their vital interests without resort to force.

Upon this decision events followed swiftly. On Sunday the Israeli Government ordered total mobilisation. On Monday, their armed forces penetrated deeply into Egypt and to the vicinity of the Suez Canal, nearly one hundred miles away. And on Tuesday, the British and French Governments delivered a twelve-hour ultimatum to Israel and Egypt—now followed up by armed attack against Egypt.

The United States was not consulted in any way about any phase of these actions. Nor were we informed of them in advance.

As it is the manifest right of any of these nations to take such decisions and actions, it is likewise our right—if our judgement so dictates—to dissent. We believe these actions to have been taken in error. For we do not accept the use of force as a wise and proper instrument for the settlement of international disputes.

We took our first measure in this action yesterday. We went to the United Nations with a request that the forces of Israel return to their own land and that hostilities in the area be brought to a close. The proposal was not adopted—because it was vetoed by Great Britain and France.

The processes of the United Nations, however, are not exhausted. It is our hope and intent that this matter will be brought before the United Nations General Assembly. There—with no veto operating—

the opinion of the world can be brought to bear in our quest for a just end to this tormenting problem.

I am ever more deeply convinced that the processes of the United Nations represent the soundest hope for peace in the world. For this very reason, I believe that the processes of the United Nations need further to be developed and strengthened. I speak particularly of increasing its ability to secure justice under international law.

48 · Letter from President Eisenhower to Sir Winston Churchill, 27 November 1956

Dear Winston,
I agree fully with the implication of your letter that . . . back of the difficulties that the free world is now experiencing lies one principal fact that none of us can afford to forget. The Soviets are the real enemy of the Western World, implacably hostile and seeking our destruction.

Many months ago it became clear that the Soviets were convinced that the mere building of mighty military machines would not necessarily accomplish their purposes, while at the same time their military effort was severely limiting their capacity for conquering the world by other means, especially economic. Unquestionably the greatest factor in turning their minds away from general war as a means of world conquest was their knowledge of America's and Britain's large and growing strength in nuclear and fission weapons.

Starting almost at the instant that Nasser took his high-handed action with respect to the Canal, I tried earnestly to keep Anthony informed of public opinion in this country and of the course that we would feel compelled to follow if there was any attempt to solve by force the problem presented to the free world through Nasser's action. I told him that we were committed to the United Nations and I particularly urged him, in a letter of July thirty first to avoid the use of force, at least until it had been proved to the world that the United Nations was incapable of handling the problem. My point was that since the struggle with Russia had obviously taken on a new tactical form, we had to be especially careful that any course of action we adopted should by its logic and justice command world respect, if not sympathy. I argued that to invade Egypt merely because that country had chosen to nationalise a company would be interpreted by the world as power politics and would raise a storm of resentment that, within the Arab states, would result in a long and dreary guerilla warfare; something of the order that the French are now experiencing in Algeria.

I have tried to make it clear that we share the opinion of the British . . . and others that . . . we would have to concert our actions in making certain that he (Nasser) did not grow to be a danger to our welfare. But for the reasons I have given above, I urged the nationalisation of the Canal Company was not the vehicle to choose for bringing about correction in this matter.

Sometime in the early part of October, all communication between ourselves on the one hand and the British and the French on the other suddenly ceased. Our intelligence showed the gradual buildup of Israeli military strength, finally reaching such a state of completion that I felt compelled on two successive days to warn that country that the United States would honor its part in the Tri-Partite Declaration of May, 1950—in short, that we would oppose clear agression by any power in the Mid-East.

But so far as Britain and France were concerned, we felt that they had deliberately excluded us from their thinking; we had no choice but to do our best to be prepared for whatever might happen.

The first news we had of the attack and of British–French plans was gained from the newspapers and we had no recourse except to assert our readiness to support the United Nations, before which body, incidentally, the British Government had itself placed the whole Suez controversy.

Now I still believe that we must keep several facts clearly before us, the first one always being that the Soviets are the real enemy and all else must be viewed against the background of that truth. The second fact is that nothing would please this country more nor, in fact, could help us more, than to see British prestige and strength renewed and rejuvenated in the Mid-East. We want those countries to trust and lean toward the Western World, not Russia. A third fact is that we want to help Britain right now particularly in its difficult fuel and financial situation, daily growing more serious.

All we have asked in order to come out openly has been a British statement that it would conform to the resolutions of the United Nations. The United Nations troops do not, in our opinion, have to be as strong as those of an invading force because any attack upon them will be an attack upon the whole United Nations and if such an act of folly were committed, I think that we could quickly settle the whole affair.

. . . I continue to believe that the safety of the Western world depends in the final analysis upon the closest possible ties between Western Europe, the American hemisphere, and as many allies as we can include to stand with us. If this incident has proved nothing else, it must have forcefully brought this truth home to us again. A chief factor in the union of the free world must be indestructible ties between the British Commonwealth and ourselves.

The only difficulty I have had in the particular instance is the fact that to me it seemed the action of the British Government was not only in violation of the basic principles by which this great combination of nations can be held together, but that even by the doctrine of expediency the invasion could not be judged as soundly conceived and skilfully executed.

So I hope that this one may be washed off the slate as soon as possible and that we can then together adopt other means of achieving our legitimate objectives in the Mid-East. Nothing saddens me more than the thought that I and my old friends of years have met a problem concerning which we do not see eye to eye. I shall never be happy until our old time closeness has been restored.

With warm regard and best wishes for your continued health.

As ever,

Ike E.

The Attitude of the United Nations

49 · Draft Resolution submitted to the Security Council by the United States[1] 30 October 1956

The Security Council

Noting that the armed forces of Israel have penetrated deeply into Egyptian territory in violation of the General Armistice Agreement between Egypt and Israel.

Expressing its grave concern at this violation of the Armistice Agreement,

1. Calls upon Israel immediately to withdraw its armed forces behind the established armistice lines;

2. Calls upon all Members:

(a) to refrain from the use of force or threat of force in the area in any manner inconsistent with the purposes of the United Nations;

(b) To assist the United Nations in ensuring the integrity of the armistice agreements;

(c) To refrain from giving any military, economic or financial assistance to Israel so long as it has not complied with this resolution;

3. Requests the Secretary-General to keep the Security Council informed on compliance with this resolution and to make whatever recommendations he deems appropriate for the maintenance of international peace and security in the area by the implementation of this and prior resolutions.

50 · General Assembly Resolution submitted by the United States

At the emergency meeting of the General Assembly, 1 November 1956, John Foster Dulles on behalf of the United States secured the passing of this draft resolution:

The General Assembly

Noting the disregard on many occasions by parties to the Israel–Arab Armistice Agreements of 1948 of the terms of such agreements, and that the armed forces of Israel have penetrated deeply into Egyptian territory in violation of the General Armistice Agreement between Egypt and Israel,

Noting that the armed forces of France and the United Kingdom are conducting military operations against Egyptian territory

Noting that traffic through the Suez Canal is now interrupted to the serious prejudice of many nations

Expressing its grave concern over these developments,

1. Urges as a matter of priority that all parties now involved in

[1]A similar resolution was submitted by the Soviet Union. In both cases it was vetoed by Britain and by France.

hostilities in the area agree to an immediate cease-fire and as part thereof halt the movement of military forces and arms into the area;

2. Urges the parties to the Armistice Agreements promptly to withdraw all forces behind the Armistice lines, to desist from raids across the Armistice lines into neighbouring territory, and to observe scrupulously the provisions of the Armistice Agreements;

3. Recommends that all Members refrain from introducing military goods into the area of hostilities and in general refrain from any acts which would delay or prevent the implementation of this resolution

4. Urges that upon cease-fire being effective steps be taken to reopen the Suez Canal and restore secure freedom of navigation;

5. Requests the Secretary-General to observe and promptly report on the compliance with this resolution to the Security Council and to the General Assembly, for such further action as they may deem appropriate in accordance with the Charter;

6. Decides to remain in emergency session pending compliance with this resolution.

51 · Resolution of the General Assembly, 4 November 1956

The General Assembly

Bearing in mind the urgent necessity of facilitating compliance with its resolution of 2 November 1956

Requests as a matter of priority, the Secretary-General to submit to it within forty-eight hours a plan for the setting up, with the consent of the nations concerned, of an emergency international United Nations Force to secure and supervise the cessation of hostilites in accordance with all the terms of the aforementioned resolution.

52 · Message to the Secretary-General from Britain, 6 November 1956

Her Majesty's Government are ordering their forces to cease fire at midnight GMT unless they are attacked.

Press and radio

53 · 'The Times'. 1 August 1956

When the Commons take up Suez tomorrow there is one thing they can be sure of. It must be their guiding thought. If Nasser is allowed to get away with his coup all the British and other Western interests in the Middle East will crumble. The modern world has suffered many acts, like Hitler's march into the Rhineland or the Stalinist overthrow of freedom in Czechoslovakia, which were claimed to be assertions of domestic sovereignty. They were, in fact, hinges of history. Nasser's seizure of the Canal Company is another such turning point. Quibbling over whether or not he was 'legally entitled' to make the grab will delight the finicky and comfort the fainthearted, but entirely misses the real issues.

The first is quite simple. Freedom of passage through the Suez Canal, in peace or war, is a prime Western interest. That freedom can be assured only if the canal is in friendly and trustworthy hands. Nasser's grab and his accompanying speeches give final proof that he is both unfriendly and untrustworthy. The second issue is no less obvious. The great oil works and fields of the Middle East are one of the main foundations of Britain's and Western Europe's industry and security. Anyone who thinks that a victory for Nasser would not encourage other extremist demands against the oilfields—and against strategic bases—should confine himself to tiddleywinks or blind man's bluff. The third issue is wider still. There can be no stability and confidence in the world so long as agreements can be scrapped with impunity.

54 · 'The Times', 27 August 1956

Escapers' Club

This brief breathing space in the Canal crisis, between the end of the London conference and the outcome of the approach to the Egyptian dictator, is a good moment to consider some of the public reactions to it. They prompt reflections that carry us far beyond Suez. When the news of Nasser's seizure of the Canal burst upon the world there was an immediate response of indignation and a determination that it should not be successful. The Governments were firm and made the issues clear. They were also admirably put by Mr Gaitskell in a balanced speech in the House of Commons (ever since, some of his colleagues have been using the balance to quote only those qualifying clauses which suit them). The seizure, said Mr Gaitskell, 'was done suddenly, without negotiation, without discussion, by force'; the episode, moreover had to be recognised as part of the struggle for the mastery of the Middle East.

'That is something which I do not feel that we can ignore. One may ask, "Why does it involve the rest of the Middle East?" It is because of the prestige issues which are involved here. I said something about prestige when I spoke in the Middle East debate some months ago, and I must refer to it now, because prestige has quite considerable effects. If Colonel Nasser's prestige is put up sufficiently and ours is put down sufficiently, the effects of that in that part of the world will be that our friends desert us because they think we are lost, and go over to Egypt.'

Mr Herbert Morrison was equally forthright. Colonel Nasser—'this pocket dictator in Cairo'—

'is not a person to be praised because he has asserted the rights of his country against this Canal, which is owned in a certain way. He is a person to be condemned because he has acted contrary to the law of nations, of international good faith.'

Mr Morrison went on to express his worry at the way in which some people, having spent many years in denouncing jingoism and imperialism in respect of Britain, and having enjoyed its advantages,

'are now spending their time in praising countries like Egypt, which are doing the very thing that Britain and other imperialist countries were doing a hundred years ago.'

It is indeed strange, and stranger still is the way in which this catch—it is hardly large enough to be called a chorus—has continued to be heard since then,

'What aggression did Nasser commit? Where did he use any force? Was he not perfectly within his rights? What is the illegality of what he has done? Are not Britain and the other Powers to blame for their past administration of the Canal? If we do anything shall we not inflame the whole of the Arab world and antagonise the East?' So it goes on, till one might almost believe it is Nasser who has been taken by surprise and is heroically resisting an act of Western aggression. Moreover, all this is symptomatic of a certain stratum of political thinking. Nearly eighty years have gone by since Disraeli castigated those 'cosmopolitan critics, men who are friends of every country save their own'. They are still with us, and unfortunately they appeal to a certain masochistic strain in our present national conscience. To these people any trouble-maker anywhere is bound automatically to have right on his side. We are asked to sanctify a Makarios; to believe that British soldiers and administrators trying to preserve law and order in any turbulent area are instinctively cruel and oppressive. Democracy undoubtedly demands vigilance. It must be sure that the men who are acting for it do not degrade its good name. Any irregularities by them must be denounced and punished. But it does not demand that prima facie they shall be believed always to be in the wrong. We may be a good people grown careless; we are not a bad people grown hardened. The truth is that it is easier to blame ourselves than anyone else. After all, there is no direct come-back in that case. It is the same mood that urges for the sake of peace and quiet we should be prepared to pour more and more millions into the maw of Mr Mintoff.

Another strange thing is the way these people define 'colonialism'. It is all a matter of water. Let Russia or China or any other Power overrun, capture, dictate to, or even destroy any of its neighbouring countries and apparently all is well. The most elementary freedoms can be exterminated, the most outrageous excesses committed. There is silence. But let Britain seek to keep law and order in some territory she is bringing along to self-government, let her say it is in the interests of the people of that territory that they should walk before they run, and at once the cry of colonialism goes up. It is true we were once a great imperial power; it is also true that few Powers in history have exercised their tutelage with a greater degree of beneficence and restraint. The day for great empires may have gone, unless they are Communist ones. But Britain's was a deliberate act of liquidation, and there is something ludicrous in the spectacle of some back-bench Labour MP arraigning Mr Lennox-Boyd as if he were Burke indicting Warren Hastings.

All this is a part of a deplorable flight from responsibility which has sapped so much of the effectiveness both of our national life and our international position. Other nations do not generally realise it is easiest for us to blame ourselves, and that while we are generally masters of understatement this does not apply where our conscience is concerned. They take these self-accusations at their face. There is a similar flight from responsibility in the constant parrot cries that everything difficult or unpleasant be referred to the United Nations. Of course, Britain believes in the United Nations. She wants to make it strong. It does no good to force it into a position where it will merely be ineffective. And so far as Suez is concerned it will presumably have first to get Nasser to obey its five-years-old resolution about Israeli shipping before it can have any confidence in going on to one about the Canal as a whole. Then there are the advocates of 'playing the crisis slowly'. They refer to Abadan. If the crisis can be *successfully* settled in that way, well and good. But Suez is not Abadan. It will be a long haul in more ways than one. And workers who have not so far understood the need to make any temporary sacrifice in their living standards to save the economy are hardly likely to be persuaded to suffer any long privation to prevent another dictator controlling a far-away strip of water about which they know little.

The last strand of irresponsibility is that which is beginning to ask whether we will, in fact, suffer in any way, whatever happens. Does the Canal really matter? Cannot we believe either that this act of Nasser's portends nothing serious, or that if it does we can sidestep all the consequences? It is part of the same thinking which produced the debilitating slogan 'Don't worry, it may never happen'. But it has happened and as, Mr Gaitskell saw, yet more will happen. Already the first tremors have been felt in Morocco. There is the blow to confidence at a moment when the under-developed countries are crying out for investment, and half-threatening to bring us down in their ruin if they do not get it. There is the fact that Russia is now a Middle Eastern Power.

It may seem to be taking these various surface waves of criticism too seriously to deal with them thus. Public opinion, despite what the dissidents angrily say, is remarkably firm. Of course, it wants to avoid the use of force. So does everyone else and we hope no one does so more than the British Government. But that is a far cry from saying that because there seems little we can do about it the best thing is to find excuses for, and forget the whole business. Nations live by the vigorous defence of their interests. Even Mr Nehru, who so conscientiously sermonises the rest of the world, does not let a trick go in Kashmir. As G. M. Trevelyan reminded us many years ago, the sun of Venice set because of the double event of the Turkish blocking of the caravan routes and the discovery of the Cape route and America. A pleasure-loving people more interested in their revels than in their responsibilities did the rest.

'During the eighteenth century the material decline of Venice was complete, accompanied by a degeneracy in public spirit that made her a by-word even in the Europe of the ancien régime. Atrophy was not, however, followed by dissolution. The corpse lived on.'

Doubtless it is good to have a flourishing tourist trade, to win Test matches, and to be regaled by photographs of Miss Diana Dors being pushed into a swimming pool. But nations do not live by circuses alone. The people, in their silent way, know this better than the critics. They still want Britain great.

55 · The 'Guardian', 1 November 1956

A Disaster

The world must be told clearly, as Mr Gaitskell said yesterday, that millions of British people are deeply shocked by the aggressive policy of the Government. Its action in attacking Egypt is a disaster of the first magnitude. It is wrong on every count—moral, military, and political. It is a severe blow to Britain's reputation, to the Atlantic alliance, to the United Nations, and, not least, to Britain's prospect of material prosperity. To recover from the disaster will take years—if, indeed, it is ever possible. The Government has ordered a military attack upon another country without just cause. Shipping through the Suez Canal had not been stopped, nor did it appear to be immediately menaced. The Israeli Government had said, truthfully or otherwise, that it was about to withdraw its raiding troops. Even if the Canal had been threatened, Britain and France were not remotely justified in acting alone against the wishes of the United Nations. Instead of upholding respect for international law and order they have undermined it. Instead of acting through the United Nations to preserve peace, as they could have done by supporting the American resolution and reaffiriming the tripartite declaration, they have treated the Security Council as useless and unfit to act. The two Governments have torn up the basis of Western policy for the past fifteen years, which has been to work for peace through the United Nations and regional alliances. In the eyes of nearly every other nation in the world, including the United States and members of the Commonwealth, they will be guilty of an atrocious act of war.

The practical consequences are hard to foresee. The Anglo-French decision seems to have been based on four assumptions—that the military campaign will be short and easy, that other Arab nations will be shocked into complying with our wishes, that the war can be limited to Egypt, and that the United States will fall into line. Each of these may prove wrong. It is greatly to be hoped that the fighting will be brief and the occupation of the Canal as bloodless as possible. But, in practice, we may find ourselves engaged in a long and costly campaign. Perhaps Colonel Nasser, if he is as astute as he seems to have been in recent weeks, will withdraw his troops and leave the pressure of world opinion to do its work. Alternatively, if the Whitehall estimate is correct, Nasser and his group will topple at once and Egypt will not resist. But by far the most likely course is a prolonged campaign, in which the British and French win an initial success but then face a long period of guerrilla and irregular warfare. Surprise and immediate strength will give us the first advantage, but beyond that stretches the nightmare of endless skirmishing and harassment. The troubles round Ismailia and Tel el-Kebir five years ago are nothing compared with what may be organised now, and they sucked in brigade after brigade merely to maintain the position. Even if the war does not spread—and there is an immense risk that it will—Britain is likely to have to mobilise more troops. The world, again, will see us chiefly as ruthless repressers.

The effect on the Arab countries, although also unpredictable, will probably be inflammatory. However little some of them may wish to accede to Nasser's leadership, they can hardly fail to support him now. That will be a damaging consequence of British action which cannot have been intended in Whitehall. Britain's oil is likely to be cut off, temporarily at least, but if that is the only physical retort we shall be lucky. There is the further danger that, since a deplorable impression of collusion between Britain and Israel has been given (rightly or wrongly), the other Arab States will take the chance to attack Israel. Let us profoundly hope they do not. They would have to reckon with British air power, which might be pitted against them. But then would Russia stand idle? There is no knowing. The explosive train has been started, and it could end anywhere. The United States has also to be considered. It must be most gravely affronted by the British and French action—and it is indeed ironic that the first British veto should have been cast against our closest ally. In British counsels it was assumed earlier in the Suez crisis that, in the last resort, the United States would fall into line with us eventually if we had to fight. It did so, after all, in two previous wars. But it may not do so this time. Perhaps more than any other nation, it must be shocked by the immorality of the Anglo-French assault. Our friends in the United States must be appalled and anguished, while those who do not love Britain or Europe will use the event to turn America away from the alliance. Whether the alliance can stand the shock remains to be seen. At worst the United States may take part in economic action through the United Nations against the offenders. At best the affront may be overcome in a few years.

Can anything be salvaged from the disaster? That depends on events in the next few days. There is a slender hope—by now exceedingly slender—that the military operation may be brief and may be followed by a standstill order from the Security Council. An opportunity might then present itself for the United States, India, and Russia to mediate. They might do so jointly or individually. It is a mercy, at least, that the United States remains as one major Western country with its reputation unsullied over Suez, and with its ability to work for reconciliation unimpaired. The hope of a negotiated settlement must now be precarious. Yet if none is reached the West may never recover. That is the measure of the task ahead of American diplomacy.

56 · The 'Guardian', 2 November 1956

Humiliation

The Prime Minister rests his case on the belief that the Anglo-French action will have prevented a greater war in the Middle East. We must hope he is right. Only time can show. But, as the Archbishop of Canterbury said yesterday, our action will leave a legacy all over the world which temporary success can never obliterate. The British and French Governments are guilty of aggression. They themselves have used war as an instrument of policy, in direct defiance of their promises in the United Nations Charter. In the process they may prove to have destroyed the United Nations—for it can hardly survive unless it takes strenuous action against them—and to have left themselves with no moral basis for future policy. And, the deepest tragedy, they could have preserved peace in the Middle East without resort to arbitrary force. They could have done it by demanding that Israel withdraw its raiders to its own territory, as the Israeli Government at first said it would do anyway, and by reaffirming the tripartite declaration. True, our troops and aircraft might still have had to fight, perhaps under less favourable conditions than to-day. But they would have been fighting on behalf of the United Nations and with the approval of most of the world, not as aggressors. The United States would have been at our side, not in anguished opposition. Now we are guilty.

The Anglo-French action cannot remotely be justified under the Charter. It is fallacious to argue, as the Government has done, that the right of self-defence includes the right to invade other countries in order to safeguard the lives of our citizens there. If that were true, China would be justified in moving into Hongkong and Malaya; and any country could invade its neighbours at the slightest opportunity. The right of self-defence applies only against threats to a country's territory or political integrity. In the Charter members undertake not to settle their disputes by force; and, as the Archbishop of Canterbury has said, they promise not to be judges in their own case. Britain and France have offended grossly. The Prime Minister says that our reoccupation of the Canal Zone is a temporary measure. But an act of war cannot be temporary; it is irrevocable, like murder. This day, for many people in Britain and perhaps also for many in France, is one of bitter shame. The humiliation is profound. At some time in the future there will be reparations to pay and atonement to be made. At present we can only hope that the military action will be as swift, bloodless, and, now that it has been begun, as successful as possible. Afterwards perhaps everyone (Britain, France, and Israel alike) may be asked to draw back within bounds, as the Archbishop of Canterbury suggests. Something of the kind is most likely to be sought by the United Nations Assembly, and our Governments should heed its decision. The immediate risk is that they may have let loose an unlimitable explosion.

57 · The 'Observer', 4 November 1956

Eden

We wish to make an apology. Five weeks ago we remarked that, although *we* knew our Government would not make a military attack in defiance of its solemn international obligations, people abroad might think otherwise. The events of last week have proved us completely wrong: if we misled ayone, at home or abroad, we apologise unreservedly. We had not realised that our Government was capable of such folly and such crookedness.

Whatever the Government now does, it cannot undo its air attacks on Egypt, made after Egypt had been invaded by Israel. It cannot undo the deliberate employment of haste so that our nearest allies had no opportunity to express disagreement. It can never live down the dishonest nature of its ultimatum, so framed that it was certain to be rejected by Egypt.

Never since 1783 has Great Britain made herself so universally disliked. That was the year in which the Government of Lord North, faced with the antagonism of almost the whole civilised world, was compelled to recognise the independence of the American Colonies. Sir Anthony Eden has the unenviable distinction of leading the first Administration since the days of George III to reach such an isolated moral position. His eighteenth-century predecessors succeeded in losing us an empire. Sir Anthony and his colleagues have already succeeded in losing us incalculable political assets.

So long as his Government represents this country, we cannot expect to have a good standing in the councils of the nations. It has attempted to prove those councils futile by rendering them futile. This is has done by, first, frustrating the Security Council of the United Nations through the use of the veto, and then by defying an overwhelming vote in the General Assembly. The Eden Government has become internationally discredited.

Ever since 1945, there have been two cardinal features of British external policy. The first has been to uphold the rule of law with special reference to the United Nations. The second has been the steady progress away from imperialism, exemplified in the full emancipation of Burma, India, Pakistan, Ceylon, West Africa and the West Indies. Neither of these cardinal features of our national policy was sincerely endorsed by the leaders of the Conservative Party, as we now see. In the eyes of the whole world, the British and French Government have acted, not as policemen, but as gangsters. It will never be possible for the present Government to convince the peoples of the Middle East and of all Asia and Africa that it has not been actively associated with France in an endeavour to reimpose nineteenth-century imperialism of the crudest kind.

In these circumstances, what should be done? Is there any way of retrieving, in some degree, the errors of the last six days? In our view, there is one essential. Sir Anthony Eden must go. His removal from the Premiership is scarcely less vital to the prospects of this country than was that of Mr Neville Chamberlain in May, 1940. Then the decision rested—as it does now—with the Conservative Party. Then, to their everlasting credit, some forty Conservative members marched through the lobby in opposition to their party leader. By their vote on that summer evening, they changed the course of British history and rescued their party from utter disgrace.

We are, of course, aware that in last week's Commons debate there was only one dissentient voice on the Conservative Benches. But this certainly does not mean that the whole Conservative Party, inside and outside Parliament, is solidly behind the Prime Minister. It is already evident that many loyal members of the party view the actions of the last week with the deepest disgust. It is for them to make their voices heard, as Mr Nutting has already done. It should be made abundantly clear that the disastrous policy upon which the Government has embarked is opposed, not only by the Opposition parties, but by a great body of Tory opinion as well.

Whether the Conservative Party can save itself from obliteration for a generation now depends on whether it produces an honest parliamentary rebellion that contributes to retrieving the national situation. But whatever the Conservative Party may do, it is essential that the world should know that the Eden Administration no longer has the nation's confidence. Unless we can find means of making that absolutely clear, we shall be individually guilty of an irresponsibility and a folly as great as that of our Government.

The Eden Administration has,

throughout this summer, shown that it does not understand the sort of world we live in. It is no longer possible to bomb countries because you fear that your trading interests will be harmed. Nowadays, a drowning man on a raft is the occasion for all shipping to be diverted to try to save him; this new feeling for the sanctity of human life is the best element in the modern world. It is the true distinction of the West. Our other distinction is our right of personal independence and responsibility in politics—a right that must be exercised.

It is for every individual in this country who is against the Government's attack on Egypt to say so by writing to his Member of Parliament, lobbying him, demonstrating in every legitimate way. Nations are said to have the governments they deserve. Let us show that we deserve better.

58 · The 'Observer', 11 November 1956

Strange Consequences

Our attempts to conduct an independent British policy in the Middle East have led to some strange consequences. The British and French twelve-hour ultimatum to Egypt (following the massive attack on Egypt by Israeli forces) and the subsequent bombing and invasion of Egypt—actions justified by references to President Nasser's book and past speeches, and now by an allegation that Russia was about to move into the area—will have profound ill effects on our real interests. They have already proved of incalculable value to Communism by diverting world attention from Russia's barbaric subjugation of Hungary. They will encourage the Arab States to look more keenly towards Russia for support, particularly since Britain and France seem to have shown an active partisanship with Israel (which will also add to the future troubles of Israel). They have lost us the confidence of Washington, where the President first heard of our ultimatum via the Press, and of the Secretary-General of the United Nations, whose resolutions and requests we ignored.

The Government now claims that the policy it has carried out at the instigation of the 'Suez group' among its supporters was really intended to further the interests of the United Nations. That institution, properly used, has proved itself capable of handling a greater danger than that presented by President Nasser, namely, the attack by the North Koreans, made with the support of both Russia and China. A method of by-passing vetoes in the Security Council was specially devised to allow this technique to be used in future cases of aggression. Why was not a two-thirds majority of the General Assembly sought to resist the Israeli attack on Egypt?

Subsequent events have proved that precisely this could have been obtained within forty-eight hours. Why did we not uphold the proved methods of the Korean experience? Had we made it clear to Israel and Egypt alike that we would do so instantly, we could have countered the aggression of either—and genuinely strengthened the United Nations. Why did we choose dubious methods which the majority of world opinion regards as having increased the risk of 'forest fires,' in the Middle East and elsewhere?

If no satisfactory answer to these questions can be given—and it has not yet been given—British policy has been culpable of an act that must weaken Britain's future influence and standing in the United Nations, the North Atlantic community and the British Commonwealth. Is it patriotic not to protest at a policy that has these serious implications?

59 · The 'Daily Herald', 1 November 1956

The Prime Minister versus Public Opinion

We are fighting an unnecessary war. Great Britain, the proud democracy which never until now in this century of slaughter has declared an aggressive war, is today involved by desperate politicians in an invasion of Egypt that can masquerade in no cloak of legality at all.

It is illegal under the United Nations Charter.

It is illegal under the Anglo-Egyptian treaty.

It is illegal under the Tripartite Pact which commits Britain and France to joint action with the United States regarding any frontier violation in the Suez Canal area.

Half the nation is unhesitatingly opposed to this power-crazy adventure. The Opposition in Parliament has registered uncompromising disapproval. Even the Government organs are irresolute.

'Boldness often pays,' ventures *The Times*. 'There must be every hope that it will do so now. Yet there are evident risks in the manner, and the timing, of the Anglo-French counter-action which cannot be ignored.'

That is not the language of a convinced and united public opinion. No wonder the Government are nervous. No wonder their brasher dogs can be persuaded to bark: 'Stop the snivelling and close the ranks.'

What a melancholy, inglorious fanfare to herald the march of modern armies into war!

A heavy responsibility is borne by those Britons who in their conscience cannot support this war.

But it is a responsibility that must be admitted, faced and justified.

An important section of the nation—and it may be the majority—owe it to their conscience to say NOW, at the most unpopular time—

This war is unnecessary, unjust, and unjustifiable.

The country is not united about its moral basis. And, judged even from the dim touchlines of political expediency, the war-game seems not worth playing.

We have allied ourselves with the one nation—France—which is clouded in Arab eyes and elsewhere as the most ruthless colonial power in Africa.

By a joint foray we have isolated ourselves from the United Nations, from the Commonwealth and from the United States.

Not a week has passed since we stood in the Security Council demanding, and obtaining, an emergency meeting to consider Russia's 'violent intervention' in Hungary.

We were champions of non-intervention. We were holy advocates of self-determination. And yet at that very moment, it now seems clear, the British and French Prime Ministers, aware of some projected action by Israel, were taking stock and making plans. . . .

They are now forced to face the American accusation that they acted in collusion with Israel to deceive the world.

That charge may quite well be untrue. But what a sorry position for a Great power, that her actions are so questionable that they bring her under the reproach of such a sordid suggestion.

Britain is isolating herself from the Commonwealth. Canada expresses deep disquiet over the invasion.

India condemns in Britain what she has so often been revolted by in others.

Colonies struggling towards freedom are learning a bitter lesson in non-intervention and self-determination.

And this country's isolation from the United States is today more deep and significant than at any time since the war.

What a personal disaster this desperate leap into battle is for the Prime Minister, Sir Anthony Eden.

In ashes around him now lies the remnant of the reputation he so painfully and honestly earned as a Foreign Minister whose constant light ahead was the rule of law.

In the great resignation speech by which he temporarily reaped political extinction—but public honour—over the entente with Mussolini in 1938, Eden said:

'It is the traditional method of diplomacy to prepare for convesations before they are formally opened. It is certainly never right to do so because one party to the negotiations intimates that it is now or never. Agreements that are worth while are never made on the basis of a threat.'

How hollow must the memory of this seem now beside his crude ultimatum to Nasser.

Has power corrupted? Has Eden forgotten that statesmen have saved their souls in the past by honest opposition to wars that expediency has advocated?

Let Eden remember Edmund Burke's noble anger against British participation in the American War of Independence:

'It is not what a lawyer tells me

I may do—but what humanity, reason and justice tell me I ought to do.'

And let the honest opposition in Britain cling to humanity, reason and justice NOW—in the face of all the vituperation they will surely receive.

The British Labour Movement and the British people have prevailed in the past when public opinion opposed tragic and brutal Government policies.

They believe today that this war is wrong—not because they love Nasser or dictatorship, but precisely because they loathe aggression and the sabre-rattling resorts of dictatorship.

They are as unwilling to condemn the people of Egypt to death and destruction as they are to wish it on our own people.

They stopped the atrocities of the Black and Tans in Ireland. They stopped intervention in Soviet Russia.

Let Eden, who has shown this week that he cares not a fig for British opinion—or for world opinion— remember the ultimate might of public opinion.

Thirty-four years ago another war was brewing, over another troubled stretch of water: the Straits of the Bosphorus.

The British Prime Minister of the day was massing troops to go to war with Turkey to deny them Constantinople.

Bob Smillie spoke then for the British Labour Movement. He said:

'Anything that organised labour can do by any means in its power should be done in order to stop this new war.'

The power of public opinion did stop that war. It is not too late for it to stir itself again.

60 · The 'Daily Sketch', 1 November 1956

Latest War Flashes

Flight-Lieut. John Slater, 34-year-old pilot of the first Canberra jet bomber over Egypt in the softening-up raids yesterday, reported: 'We seemed to hit our target O.K.

'We took them by surprise. On our way all the lights were on in Cairo.'

The Canberras, Britain's super-planes, led the British and French assault on military targets in Egypt from Cyprus. Cairo Radio claimed the city was raided twice, and other raids took place on the four key cities of Alexandria, Port Said, Ismailia and Suez. And the Egyptian spokesman said seven people were killed.

But British spokesmen in London and New York said this was not true.

Egyptian airfields were bombed and no other targets than airfields were attacked.

The Royal Navy cruiser Newfoundland has sunk an Egyptian frigate, the Admiralty announced at 1 am.

All day yesterday a military censorship in Whitehall, Paris, Nicosia and Malta blanketed any news of troops landing in the Canal area. Then at 4.30 the first British communique flashed from Nicosia. It said:

An air offensive by bomber aircraft under Allied command is at this moment being launched against military targets in Egypt—4.30 pm, Cyprus, Allied Forces Headquarters.

61 · The 'Daily Sketch', 1 November 1956

Kill this smear

The bombs are falling. The ships' guns are firing. Nasser has rejected all overtures, and so the fight is on. Let us recognise that in this drastic and necessary action, we and the French stand almost alone. We shall be assailed by reproaches even from the United States. That is to be expected, and that is to be borne.

But there is something that is not to be borne. That is the new smear that is spreading round the world. It is a smear as sticky and slimy as the track of a snail. It is worse, much worse, than the warmonger smear that brought so much shame on those who spread it.

For the new smear is this. It is said that Britain and France conspired with Israel to attack in the Sinai desert. Then Britain and France stepped in with armed forces to put an end to a war they themselves had begun.

If this smear were true, then Anthony Eden would be worse than 'a bellicose bully of a war-monger.' He would be a total hypocrite as well.

He has sent forces to the Middle-East to stop a war that might engulf the world. What respect could we have for him, what moral standing could he have in the world if he were also the very man who had started the war?

Eden's long career has been devoted to resistance to aggression and to support of international decency and the rule of law. Is it conceivable that at this late date he had betrayed all he has ever stood for?

It is not conceivable to any man of candour and common sense. But the story is spreading and will spread still further.

This smear must be answered. We must not stand idly by while our motives are blackened and maligned.

The answer to the smear can come from only one source, the Prime Minister himself. It is not only his personal honour that is assailed. It is the honour of the nation and the moral justice of our actions in this grave hour.

It may be that dark and grim days lie ahead of us, days when we will need all the resolution of a united nation standing firm in the knowledge of the justice of its cause.

We cannot tolerate that anybody should have any reason to suspect that we tricked Egypt into a conflict to secure revenge and seize back the Canal.

The Prime Minister should speak with all the conviction at his command and assert to all the world that we enter this struggle with a clear conscience.

He owes it to himself. He owes it to all of us. He owes it to the men who are fighting now.

62 · The 'New York Times', 31 October 1956

Crisis in the Middle East

With Israeli and Egyptian forces engaged in open combat in the sandy wastes of Sinai the grave situation precipitated by Israel's armed penetration into Egypt is drawing ever widening circles which reach far beyond the two immediate contestants. It is throwing into the explosive Middle Eastern cauldron not only the whole Arab–Israeli conflict but also the many other issues which have troubled that region and is bringing upon the scene not only the other Arab states but also the larger powers, with their special and not always identical interests and views.

Fortunately, for the present at least, all the powers are moving in the direction of stopping the conflict before it broadens into something even more serious, though not all are moving along the same route. Thus, following hurried consultation between Prime Minister Eden and Premier Mollet, Britain and France issued a twelve-hour ultimatum to both Israel and Egypt to halt all warlike action by land, sea and air and to withdraw their forces at least ten miles from the Suez Canal. Furthermore, they asked Egypt to agree to joint British and French occupation of key positions along the canal on a purely temporary basis in order to separate the belligerents and guarantee free passage through the canal.

At the same time the United States proposed a resolution calling on the Security Council of the United Nations to order Israel to stop what most of the delegates denounced as clear-cut aggression and to withdraw its forces from Egypt immediately. The same demand was voiced by Soviet Russia, but with a difference.

For Soviet Russia pounced upon the new developments to denounce the Israeli action as a Western plot aimed at providing a pretext for sending Western troops into the Suez zone to internationalize the canal again and demanded Security Council action to warn Britain and France against intervening. As an answer to the Soviet charges the United States resolution also called on all UN members to keep their own troops away from the danger zone, and President Eisenhower had specifically appealed to Britain and France to give the United Nations a chance to settle the controversy by peaceful means.

Last night the United States resolution was vetoed in the Security Council by Britain and France. There is no doubt that Britain and especially France would welcome a setback for Premier Nasser, the self-appointed 'hero' of the Arab world, who seek to build an Arab empire under Egyptian hegemony and exploits the French troubles in North Africa, the Suez Canal seizure and Arab hostility against

Israel to qualify for this role. Certainly continued Arab violence against Israel and continued Arab refusal to make a genuine peace are a basic factor in the situation, though this does not justify the Israeli incursion into Egypt.

A case can be made for the Anglo-French plan to send troops to the Suez Canal zone under the Three-Power declaration of 1950, which pledges Britain, France and the United States to take immediate action, both within and outside of the United Nations, to prevent violation of the existing frontiers on armistice lines. Britain could also claim re-entry into the Suez Canal zone under the agreement with Egypt regarding the zone's evacuation.

Meanwhile, however, the situation is also widening in another direction because of pledges by all Arab states, backed by mobilization of their own forces, to support Egypt. Among these Arab states are both Jordan, up to now a base of British influence in the Middle East, and, more important, Iraq, a member of the Baghdad pact. If, therefore, Iraq should feel compelled to comply with this pledge, the fate of the whole Baghdad pact, or the 'northern tier' of anti-Soviet defense, would be likewise called into question.

For all these reasons it is to be hoped that the Israeli–Egyptian conflict can still be stopped in time, and that the new shock it has sent throughout the world will give fresh impetus to efforts to establish a peace in the Middle East more solidly based than the precarious armistice agreements now prevailing in that troubled area.

63 · The 'New York Times', 1 November 1956

War in the Middle East

Despite President Eisenhower's persistent efforts to promote a peaceful solution of world problems the complex situation in the Middle East has now exploded into two related but separate military conflicts, the ultimate scope and consequence of which cannot now be foreseen. In one of these conflicts Israeli and Egyptian forces continue to fight by land, sea and air over an expanding area. In the other, following Egypt's rejection of a twelve-hour ultimatum, British and French forces have opened hostilities against Egypt for the purpose of occupying the Suez Canal and safeguarding that lifeline of Western Europe.

Both Britain and France, as well as Israel, have embarked on a military solution of their problems in the face of open disagreement with the United States and without awaiting approval of their action by the United Nations. In so doing they have given Soviet Russia a propaganda plaster with which to cover up its wounds in Eastern Europe and have aroused the other Arab states, with increasing peril to Europe's essential oil supply.

In this situation the United States has been compelled to decide on a new policy, proclaimed by President Eisenhower last night. This new policy is one of non-involvement in the present hostilities, which will have to be conducted by Britain and France without our help. We do not challenge their right to take the actions they have taken, but we also maintain our right to dissent. And we do dissent in the present instance because we regard the use of force as contrary to the principles of the United Nations and as neither a wise nor proper instrument for the settlement of international disputes.

At the same time, President Eisenhower recognizes that the actions of the three nations raise complex legal and moral problems which are not too easy to decide. For they involve the agonizing and never adequately answered question as to what, in a given situation, constitutes aggression and who the real aggressor is. In one view, aggression means a military attack across the borders of another country and those engaged in such an attack are the aggressors. In this case they would mean Israel, Britain and France. But the problem is not that simple, and the modern methods of waging war by propaganda, infiltration, subversion, sabotage and economic strangulation have further complicated it. Certainly Britain and France emphatically deny any aggression and refuse to indict Israel on such a charge, without condoning its original attack.

The reason for this attitude is that it would be ridiculous to permit Colonel Nasser to pose before the United Nations or the world as the innocent victim of aggression, or to hold a protecting hand over him. On the contrary, in so far as there is any one man guilty of aggression it is the Egyptian President. For he has waged war against Israel, Britain and France by propaganda, by gun-running, by infiltration of murderous bands, by stirring up rebellion in French North Africa, by seizing the Suez Canal by force and scrapping a treaty in the same manner in which Hitler marched into the Rhineland, by blocking the canal for Israeli shipping in defiance of United Nations orders —finally by his whole loudly proclaimed program of throwing Israel into the sea in alliance with other Arab states and creating an Arab empire under his hegemony which would expand his influence in concentric circles to all Africa and the whole Moslem world.

This program and the methods employed by Colonel Nasser are fully realized by the United States as well. Though dedicated to peaceful means, the United States has also taken repeated action to stop Nasser by invoking both moral and economic pressure, as in the case of the Aswan Dam and the Suez Canal. In this purpose, at least, the United States is therefore at one with Britain, France and Israel. And though it is now divided from them by their unilateral military action, it can still join with them in consultations to seek solutions that will achieve the common aim of all free nations.

This common aim is peace, which, as the United States has always stressed, must be peace with justice. We shall pursue this aim in the present instance by attempting to mobilise world opinion through the United Nations, including the General Assembly, to localise the conflict and then end the bloodshed. But President Eisenhower also recognises that the larger peace can be preserved and expanded only by maintaining the free world alliances, not only to cope with Nasser, but with the far more formidable Soviet empire that stands behind Nasser, and he specifically emphasizes that present differences will in no way impair our friendships with the three nations in question, nor loosen the bonds between us. To maintain these friendships and alliances is and remains the supreme goal of our foreign policy.

Extracts from Middle East Newspapers and Radio

64 · Cairo Press Comment on 31 October 1956

The Anglo-French Ultimatum
Anwar al-Sadat in ''Al Gumhouriya'

'Who has asked Mr Eden or M. Mollet for any assistance or aid? This man Eden must be right out of his mind if he thinks that Egypt will permit him to land British and French troops on Egyptian territory.

'We remember that in the first plot, of 15 September last, Eden and Mollet drew up a plan that navigation through the Canal would be stopped after the withdrawal of the pilots; the role of Britain and France would then be to come to the rescue of navigation with open interference. The whole world laughed at the result of this plot. But today Eden and Mollet are playing the same role, following their agreement with Israel that she should reach for the Suez Canal in order to create a situation which would permit them to intervene.

'In this connection two British aircraft flew over the Canal zone and the battlefield in order to report that Israeli forces had arrived at the Canal. Instead of seeing the Jews at the Canal, these aircraft were subjected to attack by an Egyptian fighter aircraft which damaged one of them. The farce is completed by the Anglo-French ultimatum, which was prepared in advance. However, Eden and Mollet overlooked the fact that the forces of the Israeli spearhead, which were scheduled to reach the Canal so that Britain and France might go to work, did not arrive at all. At the time when the ultimatum was being submitted, these forces were dead bodies on the sand.

'Mr Eden, do you want to know the opinion of the Egyptian people regarding the ultimatum devised by yourself and your accomplice Mollet? It is war to the last drop of our blood. You and your colleagues should know that this action is mean and cowardly, since you believed that Egypt was in a predicament. Egypt is determined to purge from its land the scum of humanity, to eliminate the Zionists with its own hands and without your ignoble assistance.

'You and your accomplice shall know that Egypt will not abandon even 10 millimetres, let alone 10 miles, of its own territory, as your sick imagination may have led you to believe.'

The Israeli Attack

'O Arabs, what has happened to Israel? There is no doubt that she has gone mad. She does not know what she is doing, and she does not realise the consequences of her doings. She has attacked Egypt. She is butting the Arab rock. She believes this time that she can strike, achieve a cheap victory and escape. Israel has gone mad. . . .

'Israel has gone mad because of Arab unity, which was proved by the strike of all the Arab countries in support of Algeria. Israel has gone mad because the united Arab armies in Jordan, Syria and Egypt are encircling her. Israel has gone mad because Jordan got rid of imperialism, as was done in Syria, Egypt and most of the Arab countries. Israel has gone mad, and imperialism with her. . . .

'Israel and her creators have gone mad. They wanted to defame Arabism at a time of growing Arab strength. They wanted to defame Arabism and win a cheap, cowardly victory. . . . They attacked unoccupied Egyptian posts belonging to the frontier guards, and pretended that they were fighting massed armies and (indistinct passage) Egyptian commandos and that they had penetrated Egyptian territory and reached a point 18 km from the Suez Canal. Israel has gone mad. She does not know what she is saying. . . . Israel has stated that her forces are near the Suez Canal. . . . The whole world knows that Egypt could, with a small part of her army stationed in Sinai, defeat all Israel. . . . Egypt could reach not only Tel Aviv but also the Israeli–Lebanese border the Israeli–Syrian border and the Israeli–Jordanian border. . . .

'Listen, O Arabs, to what the Israeli radio has been repeating since last evening and until this morning: "The Israeli defence forces have occupied posts inside the Sinai peninsula and 18 km from the Suez Canal". This is what the Israeli radio has been repeating since last evening and until this morning: "Israeli forces are 18 km from the Suez Canal". Where are the Israeli forces? On the banks of the Suez Canal? No. The Israeli spokesman, Israeli broadcasts and the Israeli Government can no longer dare to tell lies. Lies do not live. They must come to an end. The truth must prevail. Egypt and her army and the armies of the Arabs are the truth which has frightened Israel and made her state that her aggressive forces never reached the Suez Canal zone, in spite of the report that Israeli forces were near Suez. The denial of Israeli allegation that Israel had reached the Suez Canal was not made by the Egyptian army command or by any American, French or British source, but by Israel herself, and by the Director of the Israeli Ministry of Foreign Affairs in his statement to UP this evening. Israeli forces have therefore not come near the Suez Canal. Israeli forces therefore have not achieved any victory. . . .

'Listen, O Arabs, to the truth about Israel's attack and the truth of what happened to Israel and the truth of what is expected for Israel, not by Egypt or by any of the creators of Israel, but by Israel herself. The Director of the Israeli Ministry of Foreign Affairs told UP that the aim of the Israeli attack was to destroy the bases of Egyptian commandos in the Sinai peninsula, and that the Israeli army would withdraw to its bases as soon as the army had cleaned the commando bases. Abd al-Qadir Hatim, commenting on this allegation, stated that the frontier posts attacked by Israel were not considered commando bases. . . . Therefore there was no Suez Canal and there was no question of Israeli forces getting near the Suez Canal. There was only a defeat for Israeli forces. . . this is the truth about the attack of Israel.'

65 · Jordanian Press Comment on 2 November 1956

The Anglo-French Operations

a) '**Falastin**': Britain, France and Israel have chosen these days to strike the Arab nations because the USA is occupied with elections and Russia is entangled with the events in Hungary and Poland. The imperialists intended to deal a deadly blow to the Arab nations after the Arabs had chased them from their homeland. Therefore all Arabs should hit back, but with wisdom and sound thinking. 'Right is on our side, and the majority of nations, except for Britain, France and Israel, are with us. We should therefore act as one man in repelling the imperialists.' The Arabs must stop the flow of oil to the 'enemy, who uses this oil to fly his planes in order to bomb our Egyptian brethren'. This may not have an instant and direct effect on the present war but will be of great significance.

b) '**Al-Difa'a**': Britain has fallen to the ground because she has stooped low and linked herself with 'France, the corrupt; France of Dien Bien Phu; France, the defeated', and because her second ally, Israel, is of ill repute and hated to the death in the Middle East. Thirty-nine years after the Balfour Declaration, Britain has struck a new alliance with Israel for a come-back in the Middle East. In the future Britain will be ashamed of her disgrace and will not be able to look the Arabs straight in the eyes. 'How will Britain be able to wash her hands of this disgrace in the future? Or has Britain in a fit of desperation ceased to look to the future?

66 · Israeli Press Comment, 2 November 1956

'*Davar*': The League of Nations failed when the world was threatened with the danger of Nazism, and up to now the UN has failed before the threat of Nasirist dictatorship. The UN was incapable of ensuring the implementation of the armistice agreements and was too weak to prevent the provocations by Arab aggression against Israel. The efforts made in the UN for a peaceful settlement of the Suez dispute in accordance with international law also failed. The UN Assembly cannot overlook these regrettable facts. Only an admission of these facts can ensure the reaching of correct and realistic conclusions from the grave situation.

67 · 'Al Ahram', 2 November 1956

Total War

'We shall fight, we shall not surrender'—this is Egypt's motto today.

The sands stained with the blood of our enemy at Ras al-Nagab, al-Kuntilah, al-Tamad, al-Qasimah, Abu 'Ujaylah speak. Let this blood, which has contaminated this sacred part of the homeland, tell of the madness committed by Israel as she hurls her troops into the depths of hell!

The military actions in these areas are not war with respect to the Egyptian troops. They only mean obliteration for the enemy and a complete massacre of their troops and equipment until their allies lose their reason—those allies which sent them to their ruin.

The plan was that Israel should attack, and if she, supported by her creators, succeeded in occupying Sinai, it would have been easy for this evil gang, Britain, France, and Israel, to occupy the Suez Canal and for Israel to keep Sinai as a modest present and as a price for throwing her troops into hell!

When both Israel's allies found that they had let themselves loose at hell's gates, Britain and France joined in the war, bombing Egypt from the air, concentrating on the airports, fearful that their planes would be set upon by these death rockets, the Russian MIG's and Llynshins raids. By these raids, British and French planes wanted to pave the way for parachutist landings, but the last two days have taught these planes a lesson in war. Flown by the heroic Egyptian eagles, these heroes who are ruining the bodies and equipment of Zionists in Sinai, are themselves making British and French planes feel their hot flames. And in the battlefield Egypt's armed forces have gathered to collect their parachutists on the tongues of flames or on the tips of their bayonets.

The Egyptian Army will not be alone in this battle. Behind it there is an army of 22 million, all soldiers of the Liberation Army.

'We shall fight, we shall fight, and we shall not surrender.' This is a truth uttered by our leader President Gamal Abdel Nasser, in his speech yesterday, in which he truly expressed what is in every Egyptian's heart, male and female, every youth, every baby. All of us, on every inch of Egypt's soil, believe that this is our war, total war, on the front and behind the lines, in the deserts, in the green fields, in the villages, in the cities, in the streets, on the farms —until every aggressor, everywhere, meets a flame to burn him and an Egyptian to consume him!

This is what I was told by the thousands of youthful defenders, going to camps to take up arms in defense of their liberated land which the enemy want to occupy, in defiance of the bright future they want to blacken and the plenty which they want to reduce to poverty, degradation, and slavery.

The public has but one aim, and that is to get rid of Israel first, and then we shall meet the English and the French. We warn them that a nation which wants to live cannot be debased or scorned or enslaved or degraded again.

For if general mobilization has fulfilled all its aims and if all our human and material forces have with God's grace become co-ordinated into a strong, solid apparatus, we now need to complete it by a mobilization of morale so as to increase our contempt of rumors, always to be armed with knowledge and to have faith that we are involved in a holy war. The forces of evil fighting us fear our faith, for they have none. God has bestowed upon us arms and faith. All we need is the participation of the 'Ulama in the battle and their calls to the people: Come to the struggle.

We do not need the religious people to carry arms, but we need them to sound the call to death so that we can live!

'Abd al-'Alim al-Mahdi

68 · 'The Times of India', 2 November 1956

Imperialism on the March

In describing the Anglo-French military intervention in Egypt as the most flagrant example of naked aggression for which he could find no parallel in his many years of exprience in foreign affairs. Mr Nehru has expressed a point of view that is being unconditionally endorsed from every corner of the civilised world, reacting in horrifying indignation to the suicidal course which the Eden and Mollet Governments have chosen. In a matter about which Mr Eisenhower, Mr Bulganin, Mr Hammarskjoeld, many members of the Commonwealth, Mr Nehru and the Bandung powers are in almost complete agreement, it is possible to say categorically that the Anglo-French powers, by their undisguised violation of the UN Charter, have provoked against them the entire weight of world opinion irrespective of ideology or cold war considerations. Confronted by the fantastic situation created by the Anglo-French aggression, every member of the United Nations is under an obligation to co-operate in devising such measures as are necessary to bring about a cease-fire and the withdrawal of all foreign forces from Egyptian soil. Neither the international organisation nor—as Mr Nehru has pointed out—any self-respecting nation of Asia or Africa can demand anything less. To acquiesce in the situation which Sir Anthony and M. Mollet have forced on an unsuspecting world would be the equivalent, in Mr Eisenhower's words, of invoking 'one code of international conduct for those who oppose us and another for our friends.' If, therefore, there is a common obligation to protect the Charter from affronts of this kind, the members of the Asian-African group in addition owe it to themselves as well as to the cause of anti-colonialism immediately to undertake counter-measures against what has been universally denounced as an act of 'naked aggression.'

Since the majority of Bandung powers are also members of the international organisation and this is a matter that primarily concerns the principles of the UN Charter, it is clearly advisable that the Asian-African group should seek redress in concert with other powers through the UN Assembly. How far the General Assembly will be able to circumvent the Security Council paralysed by the French and British vetoes is problematical, but it will at least be able to place on record the 'moral judgment' of the international organisation in unqualified condemnation of what the British and French Governments have done. While there will be every agreement with Mr Nehru's demand for 'strong steps' there will equally be unanimous support for the view that such counter-measures should be of a kind that will restrict rather than enlarge the scope of conflict. It is possible for a Government, in defiance of international opinion, to pursue for a limited period a course that violates every code of decent international conduct, but the weight of combined unqualified disapproval is a force which finally no Government can resist. This disapproval—as reports from every part of the world conclusively prove—is not confined to the Asian-African powers or to the ideologically hostile communist world. It penetrates deeply into the western alliance and the Commonwealth, making nonsense of the various pacts and bonds which Britain has discarded overnight. Within Britain itself there is every indication of increasing alarm over what Mr Gaitskell has described as an assault on the basic principles of British foreign policy—the British-American alliance and the UN Charter.

The Eden Government today stands isolated not only in the international community of nations but within its own country. It is this isolation which will finally impel the Eden and Mollet Governments to relent, and it is in the degree in which counter-measures can be unanimously devised through the United Nations that Britain and France can be subjected to the pressure of such isolation. Unilateral action by any of the major powers or by any single group outside the UN can only complicate an already complicated and dangerous situation. Britain's abysmal failure is implicit in the rapidity with which world opinion has crystallised in support of Egypt and the Charter and in unqualified condemnation of the Anglo-French relapse into unashamed imperialism.

69 · 'Asahi Shimbun', (Tokyo) 2 November 1956

Again we advise England and France

Finally, England and France have begun their sea and air military action in the Suez Canal zone. An emergency session of the General Assembly has been called. This is to avoid the exercise of veto power at the Security Council and to adopt a resolution against England and France. But more important than this is how world opinion, which will be reflected in the UN, will judge the grave developments caused by England and France.

As part of the world opinion which remembers similar circumstances, we again advise England and France to order their troops to cease military actions in Egypt and to withdraw immediately.

There are many things which are hard to comprehend in the British and French action.

Whatever the reasons may have been for the British and French actions under pretense of stopping the armed conflict between Israel and Egypt, the crisis has developed because the Israeli Army invaded the Sinai peninsula and because England and France began military actions against Egypt.

British Prime Minister Eden declared that the Suez occupation was 'to separate the belligerents.' Trusting in this interpretation we thought that the British and French forces were taking action in the Sinai peninsula in order to separate the Israeli and the Egyptian forces. But the first action by British and French troops was the operational attack in the Suez Canal zone. This is contrary to the original purpose of the military understanding in the Suez zone. At the same time, the attack resulted in cutting off the Egyptian forces from the mainland and the Sinai peninsula. In this situation, the British and French are largely responsible for making the Israeli forces withdraw within their own national boundary.

France and England declared that it was their purpose to maintain freedom of navigation in the

Suez Canal. But it is logical to assume that when the Israeli forces withdrew from that area, freedom of navigation in the Canal would be maintained. Furthermore, the question of freedom of navigation in the Suez Canal should not be determined by British and French action alone. At the present time, traffic in the Suez Canal has ceased because of British and French military actions. The responsibility of England and France is grave indeed.

For the time being, the most important fact is that the British and the French are attempting to achieve their aim by military might. Such action creates serious reflection in world opinion, and particularly in the small countries. The fact that the big nations attempt accomplishment by military action is an unbearable threat to the small countries of the world which have gained their independence in recent years. As a matter of fact, it is against the current tide of world opinion. Especially it hastens the crisis within the UN because the big nations took military action after they exercised veto power in the security council.

Before the UN General Assembly adopts a resolution we hope that England and France will deal with the situation properly for the sake of the world as well as for themselves.

70 · 'Pravda', 2 November 1956

Hands off Egypt!

In defiance of the UN Charter and the principles of international law, the Anglo-French imperialists have launched an intervention against the independent Egyptian Republic in an attempt to seize by armed force the Suez Canal and to impose its occupation on Egypt. This is done at the moment when, as a result of a recent discussion of the Suez question in the Security Council, favorable conditions have been created for a peaceful solution of the problem in accordance with the wishes of the peace-loving peoples.

The Israeli attack on Egypt was but the first step in carrying out the colonizers' carefully elaborated conspiracy. Following this attack came the Anglo-French ultimatum to Egypt and a hasty movement toward the Egyptian shores of England's and France's armed forces concentrated for a long time in the eastern Mediterranean.

While the English and French diplomats were paralyzing the Security Council and preventing it from taking the necessary measures to stop the Israeli aggression, the armed forces of England and France began intervention against Egypt.

In its statement on the armed aggression against Egypt, the Soviet government vigorously condemned the aggressive acts of the governments of England, France, and Israel which are incompatible with the principles and aims of the United Nations and are a flagrant violation of the obligations assumed by the member nations of the United Nations.

The government of the Soviet Union thinks that, in the interests of preserving peace and order in the region of the Near and Middle East, the United Nations must take immediate steps for the cessation of aggressive actions toward Egypt by France and England and an immediate withdrawal of the interventionist troops from the territory of Egypt. In connection with the sabotage by England and France in the Security Council, the responsibility for the solution of this problem falls now upon the extraordinary session of the General Assembly of the UN, called by the decision of the majority of the Security Council members.

'Pravda' publishes today statements by the governments of the Russian Federated Socialist Republic, also the Kazakh, Uzbek, and Azerbaijan Union Republics, vigorously condemning the aggression committed by England, France, and Israel against Egypt and demanding that the Organisation of the United Nations take immediate and effective measures to stop the colonial plundering war.

In the name of the peoples of the Russian Federation, the Soviet of Ministers of the RFSR has vigorously condemned the armed aggression against Egypt. The peoples of the Russian Federation demand an immediate withdrawal of interventionist troops from the territory of Egypt. The government of the Kazakh Soviet Socialist Republic supports the demand of all the peace-loving peoples about the immediate cessation of aggression against Egypt. Expressing the will of the Uzbek people, the government of the Uzbek SSR resolutely condemns the faithless aggression against the Egyptian Republic. The peoples of Uzbek demand an immediate cessation of military actions against Egypt and the withdrawal of the interventionist troops from Egyptian territory. The government of Azerbaijan states that the Azerbaijan SSR adds its voice to all the countries demanding that the Organization of the United Nations take vigorous measures against the aggressors.

The peoples of Asia and Africa have succeeded in recent years in achieving great success in the struggle for their national independence. Forced to retreat under pressure of the mighty national-liberating movement which triumphed in many countries of Asia and Africa, the colonizers have not abandoned the thought of revenge.

The Anglo-French colonizers do not conceal the fact that in committing aggression against Egypt they pursue much further aims. Their schemes are not limited to attempts to seize the Suez Canal and to occupy Egyptian territory. It is a matter of direct threat to all Arab states that strive to strengthen their national independence. Moreover, the imperialist spheres of England and France defy all the peoples of the East who make a stand for their national independence and sovereignty. These circles plan to intimidate the freedom-loving peoples of Asia and Africa and to force them by fire and sword to retreat in the sacred combat for independence and peace.

But England, France, and Israel have proved to be international isolationists in the precarious adventure they undertook. Many peoples are vigorously protesting against the usurping actions of the aggressors and demand immediate withdrawal of the interventionists armed forces from Egyptian territory. All of the Arabian countries, Iraq and Pakistan, members of the Baghdad Pact, organized by the Western powers, have declared their support of Egypt.

Countries of peoples' democracy, members of the Bandung Conference condemn most emphatically the Anglo-French aggression against Egypt. Prime Minister Nehru of India qualified the intervention in Egypt as an 'insult to the Security Council and a violation of the United Nations' Charter,' as an 'astounding adventure which should be opposed by all members of the UN.' A number of other countries voiced their condemnation of the aggression against Egypt.

As has become known, the President of the Soviet of Ministers of the USSR, NA Bulganin, wrote to Prime Minister Nehru of India, pointing out that under the circumstances it would be highly desirable to call a special meeting of the participants in the Bandung Conference who might demand that England, France, and Israel immediately stop the intervention in Egypt and at once withdraw their troops from the territory of the Egyptian state. An analogous proposal is contained in a letter addressed by the President of the Presidium of the Supreme Soviet of USSR, K. E. Voroshilov, to President Sukarno of Indonesia.

The full responsibility for the perilous consequences connected with the aggressive actions against Egypt falls entirely upon the governments of England, France, and Israel, which entered upon the road of violating peace and security, upon the road of aggression. The whole world sees now the worthlessness of the imperialists' false assurances of their sham adherence to the cause of peace, their hypocritical declarations that they are allegedly concerned about the freedom and independence of nations!

The ruling circles of the state of Israel, acting as a tool of the imperialist forces, have challenged all the Arab states. Thus the reactionary and extremist circles of Israel have entered upon a very precarious course—most of all for the state of Israel itself.

The Soviet people sympathize whole-heartedly with the just and courageous struggle of the Egyptian people who defend their national independence, and they brand as disgraceful the actions of the aggressors. The Soviet people are sure that with the support of all peace-loving mankind the people of Egypt will overcome the heavy trials that have befallen them and will emerge victorious in defending their just cause.

Wrathfully the peace-loving people proclaim to the aggressors:

Hands off Egypt!

71 · Radio Statement by Walter Eytan, Israel's Foreign Minister, 30 October 1956

'The fighting which has broken out in the Sinai peninsula is the direct outcome of Egypt's war against Israel. It is nearly eight years since last there was fighting at Sinai. At that time the Egyptian army which had invaded Israel was driven back into its own territory after an ill-fated attempt at conquest. A few weeks later Egypt and Israel signed an armistice which put an end to the war. But soon Egypt was saying that the war was not at an end at all; all that had stopped was the actual fighting between armies, but every other form of warfare was legitimate.

In pursuance of this policy Egypt has continued fighting Israel to this day on every front. She has maintained a tight blockade against Israeli shipping in the Suez Canal and in the Gulf of Aqaba, in direct violation of international law. She has led the other Arab countries in their economic boycott of Israel and in every form of political and diplomatic action designed to cripple Israel and bring her to her knees.

Egypt has not rested content with pursuing this political and economic campaign, but has increasingly carried out active guerrilla operations against Israel. She has trained special murder gangs, called fida'iyin, whose aim it is to sneak into Israel to kill civilians, including women and children, and to carry out sabotage wherever they can. During the past year Israel's losses from these fida'iyin raids have been heavy. In the past week or two scarcely a day has passed without some such operation being carried out, or without Israel's defence forces intercepting these bandits and catching them before they could get at their targets. These fida'iyin raids are no partisan enterprise of a few wild army men; they are carefully planned and staged, working from a headquarters established by the Egyptian Supreme Command. The fida'iyin, highly trained, are under the direct orders of the central government. Everyone noticed that at the height of the Suez crisis, when Col. Nasser had more serious preoccupations, the fida'iyin raids slackened or stopped altogether; but as soon as there was a temporary lull in the crisis they were on again, with the fida'iyin operating at full blast.

There have been eight years of this cruel unremitting warfare. Egypt can hardly have expected Israel to take it lying down much longer. Israel, for her part, has during all these years offered peace to Egypt as to the other Arab States, and she is offering peace even now. But it must be a real peace, peace by agreement, without any boycotts or blockades, peace without murder gangs. Peace, in other words, means peace, not war on Egypt's terms. If Egypt continues to reject Israel's peace offer and continues to carry on the war in all these forms, she cannot be surprised if Israel takes her at her word. For Egypt, war means war. This is a lesson that Israel has learnt by the bitter experience of these past years. Even now, it is not too late to make peace, though Egypt seems to be as far from it as ever.

Only last week Egypt took the lead in concluding a new military alliance with Jordan and Syria, placing the Egyptian Commander-in-Chief at the head of their combined forces. This alliance was but the latest step in a campaign directed against Israel, looking to the resumption of full-scale hostilities against her.

Israel is not out to wage war or to conquer new territory. Her aim is to defend her security and the lives of her people against the constant attacks of Egyptian guerrilla forces. The Sinai desert is the place from which the fida'iyin operate. Israel is determined to wipe these bases out so that they can no longer menace her safety.

72 · Radio Statement by President Nasser, 1 November 1956

Compatriots, peace be with you, at these decisive moments in the history of our homeland I speak to each individual. At this time our thoughts turn to the homeland, its safety, its honour and dignity. Either we live a free, honest and dignified life, or we live a humiliated one. I feel and sense that each of you want to live a life enjoying freedom, honour and prestige. A life of humiliation is enslavement, and death is better than enslavement.

Brethren, let us all today think of our homeland and let the objective of each of us be to live an honourable and dignified life. This is the policy we announced, and these are the objectives in which we believed—a free, honest, and dignified life. Egypt announced her free and independent policy which emanates from her very core, and was determined to proceed along that route. All this was because of a greater objective, namely to establish a life where prosperity prevails for all the people of Egypt.

Has imperialism left us to work for this great objective, however? Imperialism has always lain in wait for us. Imperialism wanted us to be humiliated and (indistinct word) living a life divested of honour and dignity. We advocated peace and said that we were working for the prosperity of Egypt, but imperialism wanted us to work for its own ends to work so as to implement its policy. We said that we would be pacific with those who were pacific with us and hostile to those who were hostile to us, but we have no hostile intentions.

This was our clear policy, and these were the objectives we announced. Has Britain abandoned her rancour, and has Britain abandoned her cunning? Britain always lay in wait for Egypt. She stood in her way at the time of Mohammed Ali, when she realised that her armed forces had become strong, and that her armed forces had become big enough to exterminate British influence. Britain plotted against Egypt, and was able to deal Egypt a blow when she eliminated her navy at Navarino. In 1882 Britain did not want Egypt to rise and make herself a strong nation. She plotted against Egypt and was able by a trick to consolidate her foothold. This is history—our past history. Today when Egypt has become one united and fraternal, solid and co-operating bloc, will history repeat itself? What happened in the past was due to dissension and division. What happened in the past was due to laxity.

Today, we face these plots as one, one heart, one man. These plots began with the conspiracy of Britain, France and Israel. Israel suddenly on Monday 29 October began an offensive, for no reason except Britain's rancour. Our armed forces rose and did their duty with rare gallantry. Our air force did its duty with eternal courage, in the history of the homeland. When Israel attacked, Britain announced that she would not seize the opportunity. But when it appeared that Egypt was able to dominate the battle, an Anglo-French ultimatum was presented.

This ultimatum asked for a halt to the fighting—while the Israeli forces were inside Egyptian territory—the aggressor Israeli forces. It asked Egypt and Israel to withdraw 10 km from the Suez Canal. It then asked Egypt and also Israel to agree to the occupation of Port Said, Ismailia and Suez by the Anglo-French forces, for the protection of shipping in the Canal. This happened at a time when navigation was in progress and was not threatened. This happened while the Egyptian forces were concentrating to face the aggressor Israeli forces, and the Egyptian forces were repelling the Israeli forces.

In her ultimatum Britain said that if a reply was not received within 12 hours she would act to execute the ultimatum. Do we agree to the occupation by Britain and France of part of Egyptian territory? Do we willingly agree to such occupation? Or do we fight for the freedom of our homeland, for the safety of our territory, for honour and for dignity? After this ultimatum Egypt decided upon her attitude. It was this: It is impossible for her to permit, it is impossible for her to accept, and it is impossible for her to agree to the occupation of Port Said, Ismailia and Suez by foreign forces—Anglo-French—and declared that this was a violation of her freedom—the freedom, sovereignty and dignity of the Egyptian people.

And Israel—Israel, Britain's ally and France's ally—announced that she had agreed to these conditions. Naturally, Israel agreed: 10 miles or 10 km from the Canal are very far from the Canal; the (?case) would fail on Egypt's suspension of the fighting—Israel agreed, because she was the aggressor and our forces were victorious and were forcing her to retreat. The occupation of Port Said, Ismailia and Suez—naturally Israel agrees, because Israel was the only State which objected to Britain's evacuation of the Suez Canal zone in 1954.

We notified the Security Council. It held a meeting, but Britain and France made light of all international laws and the UN Charter. They made light of world public opinion, and objected to a resolution for the suspension of hostilities. Eden said that Britain did not recognise the resolutions of the Security Council, and would do everything in her power to see that Israel was not treated as an aggressor, because her act was the best of acts. The Security Council was unable to reach a decision.

Yesterday, 31 October, our forces were crushingly supreme; our air force was absolutely supreme over the Israeli air force. I am certain that all the communiques issued were sound. Our policy was to show you all the facts—our gains and our losses—because this battle is yours. Israel's losses in the air up to yesterday totalled 18 aircraft and our losses were two aircraft. Our forces, which were distributed and were massed to face the Israeli aggression, were able very quickly to group together in order to face this aggression. Yesterday, French aircraft appeared side by side with Israeli ones. Despite that our forces showed great gallantry. Our air forces (?gained) supremacy for Egypt.

At 07.00 yesterday, after the success of our air and land forces, the British Ministry of Defence issued a communique that it would bomb Egyptian airfields as a result of Egypt's rejection of the Anglo-French ultimatum addressed to her and Israel to withdraw their forces 10 miles from the borders. Naturally, the deceit in this statement is obvious. We refused to allow our country to be occupied. The statement of the British Defence Ministry that it would bomb Egyptian airfields because Egypt refused to withdraw her forces was a statement containing open and insolent lies.

Yesterday at 07.00 Britain and France began their air raids on Cairo, the Canal zone and Alexandria. The purpose of this was clear. Their raids were concentrated on our airfields with the purpose of destroying the Egyptian air force, which showed a crushing supremacy during the past two days, which dominated the battle and paralysed the Israeli air force. Thus the plan of the enemy was clear—the enemy represented in the Anglo-French-Israeli alliance. The plan was clear, and it was obvious that they intended to destroy our aircraft, to draw our forces into Sinai, to isolate them and destroy them, and then to occupy Egypt without any resistance.

A serious decision had to be taken. Should our forces be left on the borders without air cover because the French, British and Israelis were all operating against the Egyptian air force? The matter was discussed, and the military situation was discussed. A positive decision had to be taken so that the plans of Britian, France and Israel could be defeated, so that it might be possible to preserve our main forces, and so that the armed forces could always be a support for the people. The C-in-C of the armed forces, Maj.Gen. Abd al-Hakim Amir, was charged with the protection of his armed forces, was instructed to take steps to ensure that the greatest possible part of the forces joined the people, and to act for the purpose of defeating the plot of Britain, France and Israel to isolate and destroy our main forces in the Sinai Peninsula. The execution of this plan began yesterday.

And now, compatriots, that we are facing this situation, shall we fight or shall we surrender? The history of the struggle of peoples outlines the future for us. Hard days require much patience, confidence, faith and stability, so that victory may be achieved. Egypt has always declared that she will always fight in defence of her sovereignty, her freedom and her dignity. We shall fight, compatriots, the forces of injustice which want to violate our freedom. We shall fight, brethren, for Egypt's freedom and the freedom of the Egyptian people. We shall fight, as we have always said, a total war whose soldiers will be the people—the Egyptian people—side by side with their armed forces. People have fought before us against the forces of injustice which exceeded them in number and equipment and have been victorious. Yugoslavia fought German armoured units and the German air force with her puny weapons; aggressive Germany is no more, and Yugoslavia was victorious. Greece fought much greater and better equipped forces; Greece was victorious and the aggressive forces were defeated. Indonesia fought bigger and better forces, and was victorious, and the aggressive forces were defeated. And now you have brethren in Algeria, fighting bitterly against 500,000 Frenchmen, for their freedom and their dignity. And now there are fighters in Cyprus, fighting the British and French forces, which are now there, for their freedom and their independence. Your own forces were besieged for four months in Faluja during the Palestine war against the aggressive Jewish forces; they defended themselves. I was with those forces. We were called on to surrender. My answer to the Jewish officer who asked me to surrender was: 'We are now defending Egypt's honour and the honour of the Egyptian armed forces.'

We shall fight bitterly, compatriots. We shall not surrender. We shall fight in defence of Egypt's honour, freedom and dignity. Each one of you is a soldier in the National Liberation Army. Orders have been issued for the issue of arms—and we have many arms. We shall fight a bitter war. We shall fight from village to village and from place to place. Let each one of you be a soldier in the armed forces so that we may defend our honour, dignity and freedom. Let our motto be: 'We shall fight, not surrender. We shall fight, we shall fight, we shall not surrender.' Today, brethren, we are writing a new page in Egypt's history. We now need patience and faith, so that we may be victorious. I give you a pledge, brethern, that I shall fight with you for your freedom, as I promised you before, to the last drop of my blood. May God give you success. May the peace and mercy of God be with you.

The Sequel

1 · Immediate Consequences

The Suez Canal, blocked by ships sunk by deliberate Egyptian action, remained closed until April 1957 when the Egyptian government were pleased to announce its re-opening. By a curious irony the cost of its clearing was borne by all shipping going through the Canal in the form of a 3 per cent surcharge. In its own limited terms, as set out by the British Prime Minister, as an operation to protect the Canal the Suez War had clearly been a failure.

But this is to see it only through British eyes. However even for the French the problem of her Algerian rebels was left unsolved until the return to power of General de Gaulle in May 1958, when he ruthlessly cut French losses and set France free from the heavy human and financial burden of Algeria. The bitter taste left in France's mouth by the desertion of her ally (for France had been unwilling to accept the cease-fire) has taken a long time to disappear. French hostility towards Britain grew—the revived Entente of 1956 collapsed with the Anglo-French operation.

For Israel the war was completely successful. She had destroyed the Egyptian war machine, as she had in 1948, established a favourable balance of power and occupied the Sinai Peninsula. This latter success enabled her to control Sharm el Sheik, overlooking the Gulf of Aqaba and thereby to free her shipping to Eilat from danger of attack. With the Israeli occupation of Gaza the fedayeen raids from Gaza had been brought abruptly to an end. Although she reluctantly conceded to UN pressure and withdrew her forces from Egyptian territory, the Gaza frontier and Sharm el Sheik were taken over by a UN Emergency Force and Israel seemed freed from the Egyptian danger.

In the wider political sense Suez was a major disaster for Britain. Not only was Nasser not 'toppled' by the operation—on the contrary his position was strengthened and within the Middle East, in Elizabeth Monroe's phrase, Britain's 'moment' had ended. Arab nationalism, increasingly anti-Western, rallied round the triumphant figure of President Nasser and in Jordan, in the Lebanon, in Iraq, regimes once solidly pro-Western were undermined by the growth of nationalist forces.

The Soviet Union, who, at the height of the crisis was suppressing the Hungarian rising with tanks in the streets of Budapest, was able to pose as a peace-loving friend of the Arab world. Her military action in Hungary was cloaked by the great stir caused by Anglo-French action. Any moral standing Britain may have had which could be used to condemn the Russian action in Hungary was lost by her own conspiracy and use of force.

The links of the Commonwealth were strained almost to breaking point by the Suez War. No Commonwealth Prime Minister had been consulted and India and Canada in particular were extremely critical of the British action. The links held despite nineteenth century gunboat diplomacy coupled with a wildly inept leaflet campaign against Egypt.

For Sir Anthony Eden the war was a personal political tragedy. His health broke down and he retired from office early in 1957, to be succeeded by his Chancellor, Harold Macmillan, who had estimated the cost of the operation as £5 million. Macmillan, himself a convinced Suez man, was woefully wrong in his estimate. Eden later gave the figure as £100 million which was upped to £328 million by a Labour Party survey which took in such matters as loss of exports and increase in import costs. The needful connection between economics, finance and foreign policy had not been recognised by statesmen brought up in the older world of a Britain who could act first and count the cost afterwards. The disastrous run on the pound which partly brought the government to its senses was followed by petrol rationing in December, a balance of payments crisis and a massive loan from the International Monetary Fund.

One major Conservative politician, R. A. Butler, had been unenthusiastic about the whole Suez adventure but unlike Anthony Nutting, Minister of State and Britain's representative at the UN, had not resigned but had loyally supported the government. His known hostility to the Suez War however, earned the hatred of the Tory right-wing and he, too, in his failure to succeed Eden as Prime Minister might be seen as one of the many casualties of the war.

The economic effects of the closing of the Suez Canal for so many months ranged far wider than the disastrous effects upon the British economy. Many Asian and African countries, India, Burma, Pakistan, Malaysia, Kenya, Uganda, and Tanzania are concerned with traffic through the Canal. Their livelihood depends on the sale of commodities such as coffee, rice, rubber, tin and tea on the European market. They are in general committed to a modernisation of their economies which depends for its success upon the supply of capital goods from America, Europe, Japan and the Soviet Union. In 1955 over 70 per cent of India's trade went through the Canal. To force goods around the Cape increases the journey by 5,000 miles and automatically raises the price level. The immediate effect after 1956 was to allow Japan to increase her trade around the Indian Ocean. It might also be argued that any increase in costs of modernisation to countries whose populations already live at far lower standards than European peoples is a peculiarly unhappy burden to impose as a result of Britain's neo-imperialistic policies.

The dependence of the whole of the European economy upon the Middle East was symbolised by post-Suez petrol rationing in Britain. In 1955 the Middle East produced 20 per cent of the world's oil (America produces 50 per cent which she consumes herself and imports more from other producers). Oil from the Middle East to Europe comes by three possible routes: by tanker through the Canal, or round the Cape, or by pipeline to the Mediterranean coast. The Suez operation dislocated two of these routes for one of the two main pipelines had three pumping stations blown up in Syria and the blocking of the Canal meant that the greater part of Middle Eastern oil had to go round the Cape. This has in turn led to the building of giant tankers—a process speeded up by the 1967 war and the subsequent further closing of the Canal—to make for a more economical trip around the Cape.

73 · Egyptian Declaration, concerning the Suez Canal, 24 April 1957

The Government of Egypt are pleased to announce that the Suez Canal is now open for normal traffic and will thus once again serve as a link between the nations of the world in the cause of peace and prosperity.

The Government of Egypt wish to acknowledge with appreciation and gratitude the efforts of the States and peoples of the world who contributed to the restoration of the Canal for normal traffic, and of the United Nations whose exertions made it possible that the clearance of the Canal be accomplished peacefully and in a short time.

On 18 March 1957 the Government set forth in a memorandum basic principles relating to the Suez Canal and the arrangements for its operation. The memorandum contemplated a further detailed statement on the subject. In pursuance of the above, I have the honour to enclose a copy of the declaration made today by the Government of Egypt in fulfilment of their participation in the Constantinople Convention of 1888, noting their understanding of the Security Council resolution of 13 October 1956 and in line with their statements relating to it before the council.

I have the honour to invite Your Excellency's attention to the last paragraph of the declaration which provides that it will be deposited and registered with the Secretariat of the United Nations. The declaration, with the obligations therein, constitutes an international instrument and the Government of Egypt request that you kindly receive and register it accordingly.

24 April 1957

Declaration

In elaboration of the principles set forth in their memorandum dated 18 March 1957, the Government of the Republic of Egypt, in accord with the Constantinople Convention of 1888 and the Charter of the United Nations make hereby the following Declaration on the Suez Canal and the arrangements for its operation.

1. Reaffirmation of Convention

It remains the unaltered policy and firm purpose of the Government of Egypt to respect the terms and the spirit of the Constantinople Convention of 1888 and the rights and obligations arising therefrom. The Government of Egypt will continue to respect, observe and implement them.

2. Observance of the Convention and of the Charter of the United Nations.

While reaffirming their determination to respect the terms and the spirit of the Constantinople Convention of 1888 and to abide by the Charter and the principles and purposes of the United Nations, the Government of Egypt are confident that the other signatories of the said Convention and all others concerned will be guided by the same resolve.

3. Freedom of navigation, tolls, and development of the Canal

The Government of Egypt are more particularly determined:

(a) To afford and maintain free and uninterrupted navigation for all nations within the limits of and in accordance with the provisions of the Constantinople Convention of 1888;

(b) That tolls shall continue to be levied in accordance with the last agreement, concluded on 28 April 1936, between the Government of Egypt and the Suez Canal Maritime Company, and that any increase in the current rate of tolls within any twelve months, if it takes place, shall be limited to 1 per cent, any increase beyond that level to be the result of negotiations, and, failing agreement, to be settled by arbitration according to the procedure set forth in paragraph 7(b).

(c) That the Canal is maintained and developed in accordance with the progressive requirements of modern navigation and that such maintenance and development shall include the 8th and 9th Programmes of the Suez Canal Maritime Company with such improvements to them as are considered necessary.

4. Operation and Management

The Canal will be operated and managed by the autonomous Suez Canal Authority established by the Government of Egypt on 26 July 1956. The Government of Egypt are looking forward with confidence to continued co-operation with the nations of the world in advancing the usefulness of the Canal. To that end the Government of Egypt would welcome and encourage co-operation between the Suez Canal Authority and representatives of shipping and trade.

7. Discrimination and complaints relating to the Canal Code

(a) In pursuance of the principles laid down in the Constantinople Convention of 1888, the Suez Canal Authority, by the terms of its Charter, can in no case grant any vessel, company or other party any advantage or favour not accorded to other vessels, companies or parties on the same conditions.

(b) Complaints of discrimination or violation of the Canal Code shall be sought to be resolved by the complaining party by reference to the Suez Canal Authority. In the event that such a reference does not resolve the complaint, the matter may be referred, at the option of the complaining party or the Authority, to an arbitration tribunal composed of one nominee of the complaining party, one of the Authority and a third to be chosen by both. In case of disagreement such third member will be chosen by the President of the International

Court of Justice upon the application of either party.

(c) The decisions of the arbitration tribunal shall be made by a majority of its members. The decisions shall be binding upon the parties when they are rendered and they must be carried out in good faith.

8. Compensation and claims

The question of compensation and claims in connexion with the nationalisation of the Suez Canal Maritime Company shall, unless agreed between the parties concerned, be referred to arbitration in accordance with the established international practice.

9. Disputes, disagreements or differences arising out of the Convention and this Declaration

(a) Disputes or disagreements arising in respect of the Constantinople Convention of 1888 or this Declaration shall be settled in accordance with the Charter of the United nations.

(b) Differences arising between the parties to the said Convention in respect of the interpretation or the applicability of its provisions, if not otherwise resolved, will be referred to the International Court of Justice. The Government of Egypt would take the necessary steps in order to accept the compulsory jurisdiction of the International Court of Justice.

10. Status of this Declaration

The Government of Egypt make this Declaration, which re-affirms and is in full accord with the terms and spirit of the Constantinople Convention of 1888, as an expression of their desire and determination to enable the Suez Canal to be an efficient and adequate waterway linking the nations of the world and serving the cause of peace and prosperity.

This Declaration, with the obligations therein, constitutes an international instrument and will be deposited and registered with the Secretariat of the United Nations.

2 · The Summing-up

Politicians and Soldiers

74 · Sir Anthony Eden's judgement on the Arab reaction

While the majority of the United Nations was in haste to pillory France and Britain and Israel, not a mouse moved in Arab lands. As Israeli columns lunged victoriously across Sinai, and British and French sailed the Mediterranean, all was still from Morocco to the Persian Gulf. Cairo radio was successfully put out of action after a preliminary warning which avoided casualties.

75 · Sir Anthony Eden's summing-up

The factor which must now always remain unknown is the effect of a rapid advance down the canal, and its clearance, upon Nasser's position in Cairo. Militant dictators have more enemies at home than the foreigner ever dreams. It may be that even the Soviet entry into the lists would not have sufficed to save the regime in Cairo, humiliated by defeat and lacking the Voice of Egypt to call disaster victory.

I had seen the chain of failure in the nineteen-thirties from Manchuria to Danzig and had tried in vain to break it. This time we had the opportunity and responsibility. What we did was only partially effective, but it moved the United Nations to action. It led to later Anglo-American intervention in the Lebanon and Jordan, after the opposition of the United States to our Suez action had been seen to have brought disaster in Iraq. The consequences there may even have taught a little prudence in Cairo. Some of these checks to totalitarian plans may be judged late and feeble, even so they had their impact and their warning message, in revealing contrast to the fatal drift of the nineteen-thirties.

Much of the subsequent controversy over the Suez decision has been about the trees and not about the wood. The main question is whether inertia would have brought better results for the peace of the world than action. I think not. I thought and think that failure to act would have brought the worst of consequences, just as I think the world would have suffered less if Hitler had been resisted on the Rhine, in Austria or in Czechoslovakia, rather than in Poland. This will be for history to determine.

Suez was a short-term emergency operation which succeeded, and an attempt to halt a long-term deterioration, whose outcome is still uncertain. A clash between Israel and Egypt was inevitable, given Nasser's declared intentions. Whenever this took place, it could bring grave danger to the general peace. It was far better that it should not happen at a moment of Egypt's choosing, and the explosion could not have occurred in circumstances less damaging, given the speedy action of Britain and France. On balance the world stood to gain by the fact that the conflict took place then and not some months later, when the consequences in relation to world events might have been infinitely graver.

We were not successful in our wider objective; we did not bring about Arab–Israeli peace or restore international control over the Canal. It is true that some successes were gained. The military weakness of the Egyptian forces was exposed and duly noted, in particular by neighbours. This had important consequences. From the day of Egyptian defeat in the Sinai desert the chances of a Nasser empire were scotched, not killed. Even so, the Sudan did not hesitate to resist the grasping demands which Nasser later made upon her northern boundary. It is unlikely that Nasser or any other Arab leader will readily undertake a war of extermination against Israel in the immediate furture, without support from the outside. As against this, Nasser remains ruler of Egypt, his ambition still dangerous. The Canal is under his control, Syria has become part of his empire. Our intervention at least closed the chapter of complacency about the situation in the Middle East. It led to the Eisenhower Doctrine and from that to Anglo–American intervention in the following summer in Jordan and the Lebanon. It helped to show that the West was not prepared to leave the area wide open for infiltration and subversion by others. But these were only partial gains. The uneasy equipoise still continues.

76 · Mr Aneurin Bevan's speech in the House of Commons (extract) 5 December 1956

On 6 November the Prime Minister said: 'The action we took has been an essential condition for . . . a United Nations force to come into the Canal Zone itself'. That is one of the most remarkable claims of all. . . . It is, of course, exactly the same claim which might have been made, if they had thought about it in time, by Mussolini and Hitler, that they made war on the world in order to call the United Nations into being. If it were possible for bacteria to argue with each other, they would be able to say that of course their chief justification was the advancement of medical science. . . .

. . . at the end of all these discussions . . . the war aim of the Government now becomes known. . . . It was a red peril all the time. It was Russia all the time. . . . I am not for one moment seeking to justify the Russian supply of arms to Egypt. I think it was a wicked thing to do and I think it is an equally wicked thing for us to supply arms. . . . It seems to me—and here I probably shall carry Hon. Members opposite with me—that Nasser has not been behaving in the spirit of the Bandung Conference which he joined, because what he did was not to try to reduce the temperature of the cold war: what he did was to exploit it for Egypt's purposes. Therefore, Nasser's hands are not clean by any means. . . . We must not believe that because the Prime Minister is wrong Nasser is right. That is not the view of this side of the House.

What has deeply offended us is that such wrongs as Nasser has done and such faults as he has have been covered by the bigger blunders of the British Government. That is what vexes us. We are satisfied that the arts of diplomacy would have brought Nasser to where we wanted to get him, which was to agree about the free passage of ships through the Canal, on the civilised ground that a riparian nation has got no absolute rights over a great waterway like the Canal.

It has been clear to us, and it is now becoming clear to the nation, that for many months past Hon. Members opposite have been harbouring designs of this sort. One of the reasons why we could not get a civilised solution of the Cyprus problem was that the Government were harbouring designs to use Cyprus in the Middle East, unilaterally or in conjunction with France. . . . We have had all these murders and all this terror, we have had all this unfriendship over Cyprus between ourselves and Greece, and we have been held up to derision in all the world merely because we contemplated using Cyprus as a base for going it alone in the Middle East. And we did go it alone. Look at the result. . . .

The social furniture of modern society is so complicated and fragile that it cannot support the jackboot. We cannot run the processes of modern society by attempting to impose our will upon nations by armed force. If we have not learned that we have learned nothing. Therefore, from our point of view here, whatever may have been the morality of the Government's action—and about that there is no doubt—there is no doubt about its imbecility. There is not the slightest doubt that we have attempted to use methods which were bound to destroy the objectives we had and, of course, this is what we have discovered.

It has been proved over and over again now in the modern world that men and women are often prepared to put up with material losses for things that they really think worth while. It has been shown in Budapest, and it could be shown in the Middle East. That is why I beg Hon. Members to turn their backs on this most ugly chapter and realise that if we are to live in the world and are to be regarded as a decent nation, decent citizens in the world, we have to act up to different standards than the one that we have been following in the last few weeks.

I resent most bitterly this unconcern for the lives of innocent men and women. It may be that the dead in Port Said are 100, 200, or 300. If it is only one, we had no business to take it. Do Hon. Members begin to realise how this is going to revolt the world when it passes into the imagination of men and women everywhere, and in this country, that we, with eight million here in London, the biggest single civilian target in the world, with our crowded island exposed, as no other nation in the world is exposed, to the barbarism of modern weapons, we ourselves set the example.

We ourselves conscript our boys and put guns and aeroplanes in their hands and say, 'Bomb there'. Really, this is so appalling that human language can hardly describe it. And for what? The Government resorted to epic weapons for squalid and trivial ends, and that is why all through this unhappy period Ministers—all of them—have spoken and argued and debated well below their proper form—because they have been synthetic villains. They are not really villains. They have only set off on a villainous course, and they cannot even use the language of villainy.

Therefore, in conclusion, I say that it is no use Hon. Members consoling themselves that they have more support in this country than many of them feared they might have. Of course they have support in the country. They have support among many of the unthinking and unreflective who still react to traditional values, who still think that we can solve all these problems in the old ways. Of course they have. Not all the human race has grown to adult state yet. But do not let them take comfort in that thought. The Right Hon. Member for Woodford (Sir Winston Churchill) has warned them before. In the first volume of his *Second World War* he writes about the situation before the war and says this: 'Thus an Administration more disastrous than any in our history saw all its errors and shortcomings acclaimed by the nation. There was however a bill to be paid, and it took the new House of Commons nearly ten years to pay it. . . .'

77 · President Nasser's summing-up

Childers: Do you think that Suez could happen again?
Nasser: Yes, yes.
Childers: Do you really think there could be another British or French attack on Egypt?
Nasser: You know, we insist about our independence, but we feel now that they do not like that. I want to add—the United States, they do not like what we say about our independence. They do not like what we feel about the Arab countries. They do not like our insistence to be completely independent. Of course there is also the supplies of arms to Israel. The United States gave Israel two hundred tanks through Germany; then two hundred tanks through the United States; then aeroplanes, helicopters, through Germany. So Israel now is full of arms, and still the policy of Israel is to force a settlement.
Childers: You think that there might again still be an Israeli attack into Sinai?
Nasser: Yes, of course; because there is an Israeli threat continuously not only against Sinai—against Syria, against Jordan, against Lebanon.
Childers: On the question of nuclear weapons today, would you be willing to sign a non-nuclear agreement in the Middle East? For example, to open your nuclear reactors to some kind of inspection by the United Nations if the Israelis agreed to this?
Nasser: Yes, we expressed this point of view and we said we accepted the safeguards of the United Nations. Israel refused to accept the safeguards of the United Nations. I want to say again that we are willing to accept any agreement about the limitation of using any atomic weapons in the Middle East and we agree about observation by the United Nations, not by any other country. We refuse to accept observation from the United States, as this means interference in our internal affairs; but with the United Nations we accept.
Childers: Looking at one of the partners in Suez today, France—how would you estimate relations between the United Arab Republic and France today?
Nasser: We have good relations now with France.
Childers: Although relations between Israel and France continue?
Nasser: But not as in the past, not as at the time of the Fourth Republic.
Childers: What do you think British policy is towards the UAR today, and in the Arab world? Has it changed since Suez?
Nasser: British policy continues to be hostile towards the United Arab Republic, towards us. Why, I do not know. They are under impression that we are against them.
Childers: But do you think that a British government would still, today, consider trying to overthrow your government by direct force, or indirect force?
Nasser: It is not a question of overthrowing my government. It is not easy and I think it is impossible. On the other hand, they support all our enemies. Whenever they see somebody who is

hostile to us, or our enemy, they co-operate with them.
Childers: Looking back then overall, what do you think was the outcome of Suez, the effect of Suez, first on Egypt?
Nasser: We were able after Suez to nationalize all the foreign assets in our country and by that Suez regained back the wealth of the Egyptian people to be used for the interests of the Egyptian people. Then, of course, on the other hand it was clear for the Egyptian people that they could defend their country and secure the independence of their country. So we mobilized ourselves for development and raising the standards of living of the people.

78 · Ben-Gurion's summing-up

Ben-Gurion. On 28 October there was a meeting. It was Sunday. We held all the meetings on Sunday morning. It was a meeting of our Government. I gave them the reasons why we had to attack on one side the Gaza strip, on the other side the centres of the Fedayen. I told them that we must destroy the bases of the Fedayen in Sinai. And this was our aim in invading Sinai, although we did not regard Sinai as part of Egypt. Not a single Egyptian lives in Sinai—only a number of Bedouin here and there. But—I told the Government—'You will not be able to stay there because Russia and America will not let us and we cannot do anything against these two great powers. So you should not have any illusions that we are going to conquer the Sinai desert.'

This was on the morning of 28 October. We began entering Sinai the night of 29 October, the following day. In a few days we really got the whole of Sinai in our hands. The furthest place which we occupied was Sharm-el-Sheik which is near the Straits of Aqaba. And this was our main aim.

We received an ultimatum from France and England that we must retire ten miles from the Suez Canal. The same ultimatum was sent to Egypt. We agreed. We did so because from the beginning we had no intention of going into Egypt. And I told this to the Government: we have only to deal with the bases of the Fedayen in Sinai; and we would stay as long as necessary to ensure that these attacks by the Fedayen should stop. We received from the Security Council an order to stop. We replied: all right we will stop—because we were actually finished before that. No Egyptian was left inside Sinai. I think that the French and the English, especially the English, were not very happy about our acceptance of this order. They used their veto in the Security Council. Then the Assembly of the United Nations was called together. The Assembly ordered us to withdraw. We refused. We said: until we have guarantees that these attacks will not be repeated, we cannot withdraw. Secondly, until we have assurance that the freedom of navigation at least in the Aqaba Straits will be free we must stay in Sharm-el-Sheik. Then they told us that they were not sure that they could get a majority of two-thirds in the Assembly of the United Nations, that we have the right to defend ourselves by force if we are prevented from free navigation in the Aqaba Straits. The American declaration made by Cabot Lodge was not satisfactory. Then I received a letter from Eisenhower himself saying that: 'You will have no reason to regret', and that it would be all right. I knew Eisenhower before he became President. I know you can rely on his word. When I received his letter, I called the General Staff together and I explained to them the reasons why I recommended to the Government that we withdraw. When I finished, I asked one of them—who I knew had the courage to answer me even if he did not agree with me—'Are you convinced now?' He said, 'No, I am not convinced.' I asked him: 'Do you withdraw?' He said 'Of course. . . .'

Since then we have had less trouble with the Gaza strip. I do not say there was no trouble at all, but much less than we had before. So the main aims which we had in going into Sinai were achieved.

79 · General Dayan's summing-up

It may be said right away that its three major purposes were achieved: freedom of shipping for Israeli vessels in the Gulf of Aqaba; an end to the Fedayun terrorism; and a neutralisation of the threat of attack on Israel by the joint Egypt–Syria–Jordan military command.

The military victory in Sinai brought Israel not only direct gains—freedom of navigation, cessation of terrorism—but, more important, a heightened prestige among friends and enemies alike. Israel emerged as a state that would be welcomed as a valued friend and ally, and her army as the strongest in the Middle East. Friendly powers no longer looked upon her as an infant incapable of assuming responsibility for her own fate. And the sale of arms for her forces ceased to be conditional upon prior agreement among the 'Big Powers'—the United States, Britain and France.

The main change in the situation achieved by Israel, however, was manifested among her Arab neighbours. Israel's readiness to take the sword to secure her rights at sea and her safety on land, and the capacity of her army to defeat the Egyptian forces deterred the Arab rulers in the years that followed from renewing their acts of hostility. The Sinai Campaign was not intended as a preventive war. It was not meant to forestall a sickness but to cure a situation already sick—to breach an existing blockade of Israel's southern waters, and to put an end to rampant terrorism and sabotage. But in fact it did have an effect on Arab ambitions to do harm to Israel. It is not by chance that the President of Egypt, Gamal Abdel Nasser, bids the Arab States to refrain from attacking Israel as long as they have not strengthened their forces. He makes this plea not because he has stopped seeking Israel's destruction but because he has learned to respect the power of her army.

80 · Post-mortem: Anthony Nutting

Besides, the ineptitude of Britain's and France's intervention had enormously strengthened Egypt's position internationally. She now had friends everywhere; the UN were on her side; and the anger of the Arab world over Nasser's sudden decision to nationalise the Suez Canal Company without consultation with the Arab League had now melted in the warm glow of brotherhood and sympathy which had flowed from all Arab hearts when Egypt was attackd by the 'Western imperialists and their Israeli stooges'. No true Arab nationalist would now dare to resume the pressure to make concessions over the Canal issue which Iraq and Saudi Arabia had exerted before hostilities began. And all true Arab nationalists would expect Egypt to stand on her absolute rights to run the Canal in her own way and to force the West to accept her terms. Not surprisingly, therefore, after three months of abortive efforts by Britain and France, now backed by the United States, to re-establish the principle of international control, the Egyptians unilaterally announced their terms for a settlement. The Canal was to be operated and managed by the Egytian Suez Canal Authority; compensation would be paid to the former Company; tolls must be paid to the Egyptian Authority; and freedom of transit would be guaranteed in accordance with the 1888 Convention. Israeli ships would therefore still be denied passage on security grounds. And the users, whose rights to be represented in the Canal's administration had been recognised in the October agreement, were now to be left out of account. In sum, defying the insistent demands of Britain and France, the Egyptians were making sure that unfettered control of the Canal should be in their hands.

This was a bitter pill for us to swallow, and when three weeks after the Egyptian announcement the Canal was reopened to shipping on 9 April, Britain, France and America made one last effort to squeeze some concession out of Egypt on behalf of the users' interests. They advised their shipowners not to use the Canal for the time being and to continue to route their ships round the Cape of Good Hope. But when they sought to persuade other user nations to follow suit at a meeting of the Users' Association on 30 April, it soon became clear that a large majority were against attempting such a boycott. Even if it could be effective at this stage, it would be too expensive. So on 13 May the Prime Minister announced that the Government would no longer advise British shipping against using the Canal. In a subsequent debate in the House of Commons, Macmillan sought to gloss over this final surrender by saying that, in respect of the day-to-day working of the Canal, the Egyptian terms were not so very far from the Six Principles on which we had taken our stand! He also said that Britain would continue to work for an arrangement which would insulate the Canal from the politics of any one country, and he tried to make out that Nasser's negotiating position was a lot weaker than some people might think.

Historians

81 · Erskine Childers' judgement on Suez

It is perhaps necessary concisely to state what was done in Sinai and Suez. In deliberate and elaborate deception of citizens, Parliament, Commonwealth, Atlantic Allies and United Nations, a Conservative British Government embarked on planned, premeditated aggression; planned an aggression ostensibly to save that waterway but knowing that it would be ruined for months; exploited clear foreknowledge of an act of aggression by another state (Israel); and proclaimed the whole as upholding international law and morality, indeed as consonant with the United Nations Charter.

Because all this touched a catalepsy in public opinion, it is still held that all that was wrong with Suez was that it was 'bungled'. It is probable, indeed, that this 'bungled' vein of thinking saved the Conservative Party; this and the continued obsession that diverted bitterness to the man who was to have been toppled, but was not.

It needs to be stated with utmost emphasis that there was never, for a single moment, a chance that the aims of the Eden Government could be achieved. If the aggression had continued, Cairo might have been taken and Nasser imprisoned, shot or deported. A most frightful guerilla war would have continued, indefinitely.

What kind of replacement Government could have been secured? What Eden could not understand was that no political force in Egypt in 1956 could form a stable government at the behest of re-occupying Powers. Neguib, if he had even tried, which is itself doubtful, would have been overthrown. No old Wafdist leader could have even begun to hold the country. There were just two forces most likely to profit: the dormant Moslem Brotherhood (some of whose former adherents were the bravest fighters at Port Said); or Communism.

The lives and property of British and French subjects would have been placed in total jeopardy; the remarkable restraints of officialdom and populace would have disappeared in mounting violence and looting. Even this assumes that the Anglo–French forces would in fact have captured or otherwise disabled the Nasser Government.

The far more likely result of continued invasion would have been that the entire Arab world, quite literally 'from the Atlantic to the Persian Gulf' would have erupted in a cauldron of violence against every symbol of British and French authority and influence. It was, in any case, touch and go. Sir Anthony Eden and Guy Mollet came very close to lighting flames across the whole of the region, with consequences it is quite appalling to consider.

82 · Elizabeth Monroe's judgement on Suez

a)
No matter whether Eden is judged to have been carried away by an obsession, or duped by France, or merely mistaken in his judgements, the consequences of his decisions to the remainder of British power and influence in the Middle East were great, and detrimental. Defence plans were deprived of the access to Suez that he himself had so painstakingly negotiated with Egypt. Even Arabs who disliked Nasser were alienated, while Arab friends were put out of countenance; poor Nuri became in most Arab eyes not merely Britain's toady but Britain's dupe and found himself obliged to propose Britain's ejection from the Baghdad Pact. Jordan dismissed the few British officers still serving with its forces, and abrogated the Anglo–Jordanian Treaty. As for oil, its transit was stopped not only by Nasser's blockships in the Suez Canal, but by the Arab states that controlled the trans-desert pipelines. The Syrians blew up the pumping stations on the lines from Iraq, and the Saudi Government forbade pumping to British-held terminals, or into British ships. (Ironically the first multiple Arab action taken to apply the oil sanction that had often been discussed was precipitated by British action, and directed at Great Britain.) The Soviet Government, which on November 5 brandished rockets at London, was enabled to drive all thought of Hungary out of Arab minds, and momentarily to assume in Arab eyes the role of a savior who had brought about the British cease-fire order of the next day, and the Anglo–French withdrawal. The President of the United States was made a gift of an anti-imperialist cause carrying no risk of electoral embarrassment. Not even Israel was pleased; by its standards Mollet and Eden had robbed it of its chance of bringing Nasser down for ever.

The Suez adventure put an end to British influence in all the more important countries of the Arab world except Iraq, and there the respite was short. At all points (except in Baghdad while Nuri Pasha's regime survived, and in the deep south made up of the Aden dependencies and the Arab principalities of the Persian Gulf) Britain's hold on events ceased, and remained at zero while the free world gasped at so radical a departure from British principle and practice. Asians and Africans were dumbfounded not so much at the act of dropping bombs on Nasser, for many victims of Egypt's radio invective felt that he had asked for trouble, but at British exercise of the veto at the United Nations on an injunction to cease fire.

b)

Diplomatic and military plans must be judged by the degrees to which they stand up to contemporary conditions, including unexpected conditions. A plan that is thrown out of joint by a change of date is faulty, and no plan is a good plan if it produces three of the worst mistakes a government can make—miscalculation of world opinion, bad military timing, and choice of an inconvenient ally. When the Anglo–French landing craft finally chugged ashore on 5–6 November, these three handicaps had between them wrecked all chance of presenting the Anglo–French forces as knight-errants making the Suez Canal safe for the world. In the meantime, Egypt had seen which way the wind of international opinion was blowing, and had used the one conclusive weapon at its disposal; it had sunk ships in the Canal, and blocked it.

The rest of the tale of British action is soon told—military clockwork, negligible British casualties, the order to halt when only half of the blocked Canal had been occupied. One reason for the order, given on the day of the landing, was a volume of international and domestic pressure to desist that was not merely moral and diplomatic, but financial. A decisive reason for going into reverse was a disastrous run on the pound sterling that threatened the whole fabric of confidence in Britain that underpins the sterling area. No Chancellor of the Exchequer could afford to ignore the danger signals, or fail to recommend saving the pound by reversing the policy. The adventure was a failure; most members of the British Cabinet recognised it to be so; they decided to yield to the United Nations; Eden collapsed.

83 · Hugh Thomas's summing-up

The consequences of Suez were different from the predictions of both those who backed the operation and those who condemned it. Thus instead of the American alliance being broken, the British had never been able since to venture on a foreign policy independent of the USA. It was the Entente Cordiale that broke, which thus died, as it was born, over Egypt. Suez was partly responsible both for Gaullist diplomacy and for the end of the Fourth Republic. At the same time, Suez failed both to give the UN military substance, as the Conservatives claimed desperately in the closing hours of the military action to be at least one lasting achievement, and to destroy it, as Labour predicted. The Commonwealth undoubtedly took a harsh blow from the lack of consultation, and it would be doubtless not the same again in the event of another world war; but it has staggered on, changed more by other things. A 'Suez reflex' doubtless affected Labour ministers over Rhodesia in 1965, just as a 'Munich reflex' affected their predecessors in 1956.

Nor did Suez prove that Britain was unable to take any military action without the USA: only that we could not do so while maintaining a reserve currency and needing to rely on the USA both for oil and for ultimate protection against 'the Bear'.

The Anglo–French invasion of Egypt at that point was the one act of international policy which was able to give victories to both Egypt and Israel: Egypt got the Canal and victory over 'imperialism'; Israel freed the Gulf of Aqaba, destroyed the Fedayun bases in Gaza and ruined Egyptian military prestige. It was a fitting conclusion, for both Nasser and Ben-Gurion had outplayed the statesmen of old Europe in guile and resolution. Nasser, unlike Russia, understood (doubtless through the agency of the US ambassador, Byroade) that US policy and Anglo–French policy were not the same. A major war between Egypt and Israel, on the cards early in 1956, was thus staved off, at the cost of not much more than 3,000 lives.

But it is impossible to believe that, even if the benevolent connivance of the USA had been ensured beforehand, any re-establishment of Anglo–French power could have been permanently achieved in the Middle East by the use of force. The faith that the Governments seem to have had in Nahas Pashà and that Britain still had in Nuri es-Said are evidence of a certain unreality, or romanticism, in their approach to these matters. In simple terms of realpolitik, the situation would have been different if we had had the physical power. But we did not. If the only settlement of the problems of the Middle East that was acceptable to the Governments of Britain and France meant that the armed forces of these countries would have to re-occupy parts of Egypt, if there had followed longer periods of rule by Western puppets, then hatreds in the region would obviously have swollen; Russia would really have been 'let into Africa'; Israel's fate would have been even more unpredictable; and the British and French peoples would surely have had to face a prolonged time of sabotage of their oil supplies, thrusting them completely into the hands of the USA to maintain their economies at all. Other economic difficulties would perhaps have brought impoverishment.

Of course, the Suez expedition was popular at home among many people for a time; so was Alcibiades' expedition to Sicily, before it left Athens. Of course the French, having embarked upon a policy of repression in Algeria, had everything to gain from drawing Britain into their debilitating conflict. But it is impossible to believe that France could eventually have avoided conceding the independence of Algeria. For all these reasons the whole idea of a 'great expedition', to restore national pride as well as to internationalise the Canal, appears, again like that of Alcibiades, to have been doomed from the start.

3 · The Six Days War : 1967

Israel in 1956 was an ally of two great Western powers. Her war had a radically different purpose from that of Britain and France: she was helped to total victory by Anglo-French air power and by France's sale to her of Mystères and Mirages. In 1956 Israel struck at a relatively unprepared Egypt determined to destroy the fedayeen marauders and to right the balance of power so dangerously tilted against her after the Egypt–Czech arms deal.

In 1967 the fedayeen raiders, trained and based upon the Gaza Strip, had ceased to operate. However a potentially more dangerous guerilla force, the Fatah, had been created from Palestinian Arabs committed to exacerbating relations between Arabs and Israel to such a point that open war would follow. The Fatah, trained in Syria, infiltrated Jordan and carried out raids from Jordanian territory. The Fatah had its political theorists who looked to the Vietcong as a model and left-wing socialism as a guide.

In 1967 Israel had no ally, even de Gaulle had proved unfriendly, and the Arab armies were far from unready. On every Israeli front, Sinai, the West Bank, Syria, Arab armies were massed. Yet within six days, almost within the first day, Israel had proved victorious. So much so that Nasser at first propagated the myth that Israel had powerful allies. In his account of Arab–Israeli relations, *Palestine, the Arabs and Israel* Henry Cattan credits Eshkol and the Israelis with Bismarckian cunning. By announcing the closure of the Straits of Tiran to Israeli shipping, Egypt fell into the trap and gave Israel the pretext she had been waiting for. On the morning of 5 June 1967 Israel struck with savage force. . . . The two million Israelis had manouevred the 100 million Arabs into a corner.

The truth is far more complex. Certainly 1967 may be seen as another phase of the Israel–Arab conflict and in many ways a direct consequence of the 1956 war. It is more difficult to see the 1967 war as part of an Israeli plan to seize on the right moment for a war of expansion and destruction.

One major factor in the situation was the new Baath government in Syria, the most extreme and bellicose in the whole of the Middle East, which over its radio proclaimed to Israel 'we have decided to drench this land with our blood, to oust you, aggressors, and throw you into the sea for good'. Not only did Syria nurture the Fatah but during 1966–7 fired almost daily at Israeli settlements. Israel, in line with her policy of massive retaliation, replied to this with a heavy and ill-judged raid on Samu, in Jordan, on 13 November 1966, to punish the village harbouring terrorists by destroying its houses. The Israeli force found itself engaged by the Jordan Arab Legion and an open battle ensued. Within Jordan, the Samu raid produced demands for a tougher policy towards Israel and helped to persuade the moderate Hussein that Samu implied the beginning of Israeli expansion towards the West Bank.

Israel–Syrian relations continued to deteriorate and on 7 April 1967 the Israelis carried out a massive attack on Syria. They shot up Syrian guns attacking Israeli settlements and then shot down six Syrian Mig 21s. Nevertheless Syrian activity continued and on 11 May Prime Minister Eshkol publicly warned Syria that unless Syria stopped these attacks Israel would strike back hard. In this mounting tension, Russia intervened and informed Syria and Egypt that Israel intended to attack Syria on 17 May. This non-existent war plot may well have been the pivot of all that followed for on 14 May Nasser began the mobilisation of the Egyptian army—he had decided to go to the assistance of the Syrians.

From this point onwards the crisis escalated. On 16 May Nasser took the precipitous step of ordering the UN Emergency Force to leave Egyptian territory and the UN Secretary-General promptly agreed. The UNEF forces at Sharm-el-Sheik had implicitly guaranteed safety to Israeli shipping using the growing port of Eilat: this protection was now withdrawn. On 23 May Nasser took the warlike step of closing the Tiran straits against Israeli shipping. At the same time Egyptian armour massed along the Israeli border in Sinai. Was the whole purpose of this large scale operation to deter the Israelis from any attack on Syria? Certainly this may have been the original intention but now the Egyptian mood was euphoric. Speaking to the National Assembly on 29 May Nasser said 'We are now ready to confront Israel . . . we are now ready to deal with the entire Palestine question'. In Iraq, the President informed his troops 'we are determined to achieve our clear aim—to remove Israel from the map'.

The Jordanian ruler then agreed to the entry of Iraqui and Saudi Arabian troops into Jordan. On 30 May Hussein followed this by a surprise visit to Cairo where he signed a military pact with Nasser, who had for so long allowed his propagandists to dub Hussein 'the running dog of imperialism'.

In Israel hawks and doves contested policy. Outside Israel and the Middle East there was a sad-sick feeling that in Field Marshal Montgomery's words in 1948 'the Jews had bought it'. For once the Arab world was totally united and the propaganda dread of twenty years was about to be realised: Israel was to disappear from the map. Even in the Lebanon, traditionally peaceful, the armed forces were at the ready.

On 5 May the Israelis struck. Ringed around by Arab armies Dayan and his hawkish policies won the day. By the close of the first day the Arab airforce had been destroyed and on every Arab front in turn the Israelis were victorious—at the armistice, the armies occupied the West Bank, Sinai, the Golan Heights in Syria commanding the Israeli border settlements and the Old City of Jerusalem. The sequel to 1956 was total disaster to the Arab world: Israel had now expanded; the balance of power had tilted drastically in her favour; her frontiers were now infinitely more defensible than in 1956.

Appendix

Some Issues

The Three Crises

Three major crises occurred in October/November 1956. The first was a crisis in British history as her government embarked on policies strikingly out of key with her enlightened attitude to India and Africa and representing an attitude to politics which might fairly be called latter-day imperialist. (This was not true of France who had been fighting rearguard actions in her empire for some years and the Suez operation, for her, was an extension of her colonial policies.) The second crisis was a phase of the long drawn out crisis of Arab–Israeli relations. The Anglo–French decision to use Israel brought a temporary fusion in these two crises. The third, the tragedy of the brutal Russian suppression of the Hungarian rising has hardly a mention in this book. And indeed in the world press of 2 November (as W. L. Schramm has shown in *One Day in the World's Press*) Suez overshadowed Hungary in coverage. The world turned towards the British and French aggressors and largely ignored the Russian action in Budapest. Against the background of Russian tanks prowling in the streets of the Hungarian capital, Russian threats to Britain have a curious self-righteousness (pp 68–70).

A study of the documents will reveal not only the depth of the crisis and its causes but also throw up problems of politics and political behaviour which are of perennial interest. This brief note can only serve to suggest a few of those problems.

What was the importance of the nationalisation of the Canal?

It might be answered simply that nationalisation helped to trigger off the crisis and to exacerbate British and French feelings. But on Nasser's action hinges a whole series of other questions. The Canal had been built largely by foreign capital and skills. How far does a commercial country have a continuing right to make profits from a long term investment of this kind, particularly when the presence of the Canal on Egyptian territory must carry with it the presence of foreign technicians, pilots and managers. How important were the rights of shareholders when Nasser nationalised the Canal? Was it the manner of his action, its abruptness and lack of prior negotiation which was at fault rather than the fact of nationalisation itself? (pp 33–39)

How did the cold war affect the situation?

Was Egypt's purchase of arms from Czechoslovakia a policy decision to align Egypt with the Soviet bloc or was it as Nasser says no more than a commercial decision (p. 0)? If it was a commercial decision was there any way in which America and the Western Powers could appreciate this? Can the purchase of technological devices on a large scale ever be independent of 'influence' in terms of advisers, technicians, the continuing purchase of spares and replacements? Was Nasser right in his insistence and the West equally right in theirs? Was the attitude of John Foster Dulles, the American Secretary of State, in any way responsible? (pp 19, 29).

Why did Israel attack?

Israel in 1956 was the aggressor and her statesmen give explanations sufficient for her action (pp 22–24, 94). But is an offensive/defensive war ever justified? and if so, in what circumstances? Does this war turn basically on the refusal of the Arabs to recognise the political fact of the existence of Israel? Should the Arabs recognise Israel? or is their view that Israel is an imposition of Western imperialism, an outpost of Western colonialism in the undeveloped Middle East in line with the facts of Israel's birth? Even if there is justice in this view, is it practical politics, faced by a militant and technically efficient Israel? Are Arab threats so blood-thirsty as to make Israel desperate in her determination to survive?

Why did Britain intervene?

The British explanation for her intervention (pp 57, 105) has since been largely discredited (pp 53–55). How far were British ministers justified in hiding their true motives? Did Britain's relationship with oil-producing Middle Eastern countries make this necessary? Was she in this sense forced to hide her arrangements with Israel?

Certainly, even with this calculation in mind, there was little accurate assessment of the economic consequences of Suez. The dramatic effects of the loss of oil supplies, the increased cost of transport round the Cape, the shift in the balance of payments, all these were severe blows to the British economy. Furthermore these economic ill-effects were not limited to the participants but affected countries remote from these events. How far should foreign policy be weighed against cost? Is there a point beyond which the cost of the operation should be disregarded? What gains could the Suez operation bring to offset economic loss?

Why was the British government so blind to the repercussions of world opinion?

Clearly in the Suez operation Britain had few friends left in the world. Stalwarts in the Arab lands like Jordan turned against her. Ex-colonial nations everywhere saw Suez as a potential threat against themselves. Old friends such as America and Canada, Commonwealth countries such as India were uniformly hostile. Why had Britain disregarded the attitude of other friendly states? Was she simply uncaring or was this a fundamental misjudgement of possible reactions? (pp 73–75).

On what grounds, if any, is intervention in the domestic affairs of another country justifiable?

Eden saw his action as a moral duty, a further blow struck in the defence of liberty and against dictatorship. Appeasement—the conciliation of Hitler in the Thirties—had nearly produced a Nazi domination of Europe. In Eden's view, appeasing Hitler was morally wrong and politically disastrous. To appease Nasser was just as undesirable. Britain intervened to 'topple' Nasser. Was Suez, then, an example of wrongly applying the doctrine of intervention? Is intervention in the domestic affairs of another country ever justifiable? to prop up friendly régimes? to avoid a hostile coup? to prevent genocide? to protect property and 'British interests'? Was 1956 perhaps an example of bad historical thinking? the use of inappropriate historical analogies?

What was the role of the United Nations?

Why did the British, French and Israeli governments act outside the framework of the UN? What was the UN function at the height of the crisis? Would you regard the setting up of the United Nations Emergency Force as the one positive gain from the crisis? Where were they stationed? and what importance did they have in 1967? (pp 75–76, 115–116).

1956 saw four nations at war to protect their own 'interest'. Does the Suez affair underline once again the need for a strong impartial authority to decide between conflicting parties? or in the Middle East with nationalism strident is there much hope that an impartial authority, if it could be established, would ever be accepted?

Glossary

Arab League: Loose organisation of Arab states.

Bandung Conference: Conference of uncommitted states held in 1955 and attended by (amongst others) Nehru, Chou-en-lai and Nasser.
Its purpose was to find a third way, independent of the Soviet Union and the USA.

Bevan, Aneurin: Leader of the Labour left, one of the great orators in the Commons. MP for Ebbw Vale.

Ben-Gurion, David: Israel Prime Minister at the time of the Sinai Campaign, a founding father of Israel, an advocate of a hawkish line against the Arabs.

Bulganin, Marshal: in 1956, together with Krushchev, one of the two rulers of the Soviet Union.

Burns E. L. M., Lieutenant-General: Canadian officer responsible for UNTSO (United Nations Truce Supervisory Organisation). UNTSO concerned itself with the whole range of Arab–Israeli frontier disputes and reported to the UN.

Challe, General Maurice: Chief of the French Air Staff.

Dayan, General Moshe: Israeli Chief of Staff.

Dulles, John Foster: American Secretary of State, profoundly concerned with Communist peril, an exponent of the Cold War.

Eban, Abba: Israeli Ambassador to the USA in 1956, now Israel's Foreign Minister.

Gaitskell, Hugh: Leader of Her Majesty's Opposition and Leader of the Labour Party.

Gazier, Albert: junior minister in the French government.

Lloyd, Selwyn: British Foreign Minister.

Menzies, Sir Robert: Australian Prime Minster and strong supporter of British policy towards Egypt.

Mintoff, Dominic: Prime Minister of Malta.

Morrison, Herbert: Elder Statesman of the Labour Party.

Mollet, Guy: French Prime Minister.

Moslem Brotherhood: Fanatical Egyptian right-wing group, particularly active in the late 'forties in Egypt.

Nahas, Pasha: 80 year old Egyptian politician, strongly pro-British and thought by the British to be the obvious successor to Nasser.

Nasser, Gamal Abdel: President of Egypt, organiser of the officer's plot of 1952 which disseated King Farouk.

Nuri-al-Said: Pro-British Prime Minister of Iraq, murdered in the 1958 army coup.

Nutting, Anthony: Minister of State and British representative at UN who resigned in opposition to Suez on 4 November.

Pineau, Christian: French Foreign Minister.

Sharett, Moshe: Israel's Prime Minister until the eve of the Sinai Campaign.

Shepilov, Dmitri Trofimovitch: Soviet Foreign Minister.

Sources of Documents

1 M. Khalil: *The Arab States and the Arab League*, Vol. 2 Khayats Beirut
2 *Suez Canal: Annual Returns of Shipping and Tonnage*, HMSO 1956
3 Hurewitz: *Diplomacy in the Near and Middle East*, Nostrand, Princeton
4 Hurewitz, *op cit*
5 Hurewitz, *op cit*
6 Hurewitz, *op cit*
7 Hurewitz, *op cit*
8 General Dayan: *Diary of the Sinai Campaign*, Weidenfeld and Nicolson, 1966
9 Sayegh, F. H.: *Zionist Colonialism in Palestine*, Palestine Liberation Organisation (Publishers), Beirut, 1955
10 Department of State Bulletin, 17 December 1955 Vol. 33
11 Department of State Bulletin, 19 July 1955, Vol. 35
12 Finer, Herman: *Dulles Over Suez*, Heinemann
13 R.I.I.A. Vol. for 1956
14 R.I.I.A. Vol. for 1956
15 R.I.I.A. Vol. for 1956
16 Hansard Vol. 557, coll. 777–80
17 Hansard Vol. 557, Coll. 1609–17
18 Sir Anthony Eden: *Full Circle*, Cassell 1960
19 R.I.A.A. Vol. for 1956
20 Eden, *op cit*
21 Hansard Vol. 558, coll. 10–15
22 R.I.A.A. Vol. for 1956
23 Eden, *op cit*
24 Eden, *op cit*
25 Nutting, Anthony: *No End of a Lesson*, Constable 1967
26 Eden, *op cit*
27 Nutting, *op cit*
28 Thomas, Hugh: *The Suez Affair*, Weidenfeld and Nicholson 1966
29 Dayan, *op cit*
30 Burns, E. M. L.: *Between Arab and Israeli*, Harrap 1962
31 Dayan, *op cit*
32 Eden, *op cit*
33 R.I.A.A. Vol. for 1956
34 Hansard Vol. 558 coll. 1648–69
35 Eayrs: *The Commonwealth and Suez*, O.U.P., 1964
36 Gale, J.: *Clean Young Englishman*, Hodder & Stoughton 1969
37 Barer, S.: The Weekend War, Yoseloff, London 1959
38 *The New Statesman*, 29 December 1956
39 Eden, *op cit*
40 *The Spectator*, 19 December 1956
41 Eden, *op cit*
42 R.I.A.A. Vol. for 1956
43 R.I.A.A. Vol. for 1956
44 *Soviet News* 1 November 1956
45 R.I.A.A. Vol. for 1956
46 R.I.A.A. Vol. for 1956
47 R.I.A.A. Vol. for 1956
48 *Public Papers of the Presidents of the United States—Dwight D. Eisenhower, 1956*, published by the National Archives and Records Service, 665.5b.5.12.
49 R.I.A.A. Vol. for 1956
50 Eisenhower, D. D. *Waging Peace*, Heinemann 1966
51 R.I.A.A. Vol. for 1956
52 R.I.A.A. Vol. for 1956
53 *The Times*, 1 August 1956
54 *The Times*, 27 August 1956
55 *The Guardian*, 1 November 1956
56 *The Guardian*, 2 November 1956
57 The *Observer*, 4 November 1956
58 The *Observer*, 11 November 1956
59 The *Daily Herald*, 1 November 1956
60 The *Daily Sketch*, 1 November 1956
61 The *Daily Sketch*, 1 November 1956
62 The *New York Times*, 31 October 1956
63 The *New York Times*, 1 November 1956
64 Excerpts from broadcast Press comment: Cairo in Arabic Home Service, 0600 GMT 31 October 1956.
65 Excerpts from broadcast press comment: Jerusalem (Ramallah) in Arabic 05.55 GMT, 2 November 1956.
66 Excerpt from broadcast press comment; Jerusalem radio 2 November 1956
67 Schramm, W.: *One Day in the World's Press*, Stanford University Press, 1959
68 Schramm, *op cit*
69 Schramm, *op cit*
70 Schramm, *op cit*
71 Israel in English 'Voice of Zion' 21.30, 30 October 1956
72 Cairo in Arabíc Home Service, 13.10. GT, 1 November 1956
73 *Dept. of State Bulletin*, 24th April 1957
74 Eden, *op cit*
75 Eden, *op cit*
76 Harsard, Vol. 561, Coll. 1267–87
77 Broadcast made by Peter Calvocoressi (extract), 7 July 1966. Published in *Suez Ten Years After*, BBC, 1967
78 Calvocoressi, *op cit*
79 Dayan, *op cit*
80 Nutting, *op cit*
81 Childers, E.: *Judgement on Suez*
82 Monroe, E.: *Britain's moment in the Middle East*
83 Thomas, *op cit*

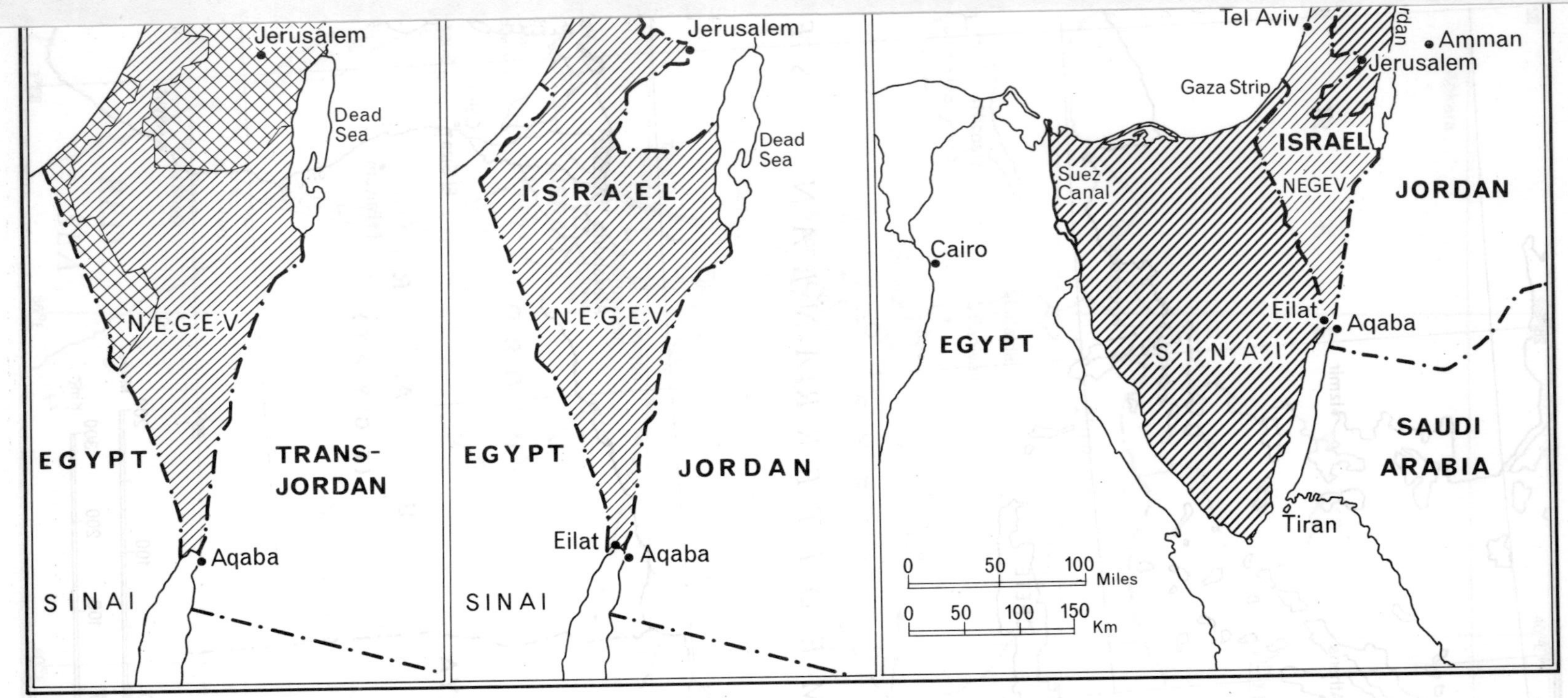

The changing border of Israel 1947–67